B-ism-Allah, Al-Rahman, Al-Raheem
In the name of God, The Compassionate, The Merciful

MARCH FORTH

FROM THE PRISON OF MINDS

MEDINA MEDIA
PUBLISHING

MEDINA MEDIA
PUBLISHING

Medina Media Publishing is a division of Medina Media, LLC
Dearborn, MI
Book cover by *semnitz*™
Interior design by Rafael Andres
Printed in the United States of America
Hardcover ISBN: 979-8-9897345-0-4

Author's Note

I co-authored this book with my Baba, Sayyed Imad Mahmoud Fadlallah. May Allah—the Most Glorified, the Most Exalted—rest his soul and grant him paradise.

Five chapters—1, 2, 5, 6, and 10—and part of the epilogue were written by him.

The remaining pages were written by me with hopes of portraying the true nature of my transition from a Fordson boy—trapped in a prison of ignorance—to a Muslim man: humbled by God's mercy, inspired by Baba's leadership, and enlightened by the truth of our beloved Prophet (s), his Holy Progeny (as), and the immaculate religion of Islam. Any success in my efforts to illustrate this journey is a credit to our Creator, while any shortcomings are my own.

Pseudonyms were used to hide the identities of many individuals, some of whom were victims or victimizers. Many of these victimizers remain in power today.

أَنفِرُواْ خِفَافًا وَثِقَـالًا وَجَـٰهِدُواْ بِأَمْوَٰلِكُمْ وَأَنفُسِكُمْ
فِى سَبِيلِ ٱللَّهِ ذَٰلِكُمْ خَيْرٌ لَّكُمْ إِن كُنتُمْ تَعْلَمُونَ

"March forth, whether it is easy or difficult for you, and strive with your wealth and your lives in the cause of Allah. That is best for you, if only you knew."

-The Holy Quran, 9:41

PROLOGUE

GROUND ZERO

0. GROUND ZERO

2004

Junior year. Typical lunch hour. I'm trying to maneuver Mama's metallic-gold Tahoe from Fordson's parking lot to JT's Pizza, where two halal pepperoni slices and perfect-recipe ranch await me, when suddenly, the new kid walks in front of the truck without even glancing to make sure I stop. I slam my brakes, staring down on what looks like a Black versus Arab gang scene in an unwritten film: the new kid and Ali Alaguli walking toward one another, each with a crew of boys trailing left and right like a flock of birds. The kid lifts his shirt to flash a Glock. Then he grabs it and points it at Alaguli—the only other Ali ibn[1] Imad I know of, but clearly a different breed.

With his loose screw and bruised knuckles, Alaguli calls bluff on the bullet, letting out a bizarre growl as he charges at the boy, landing a right hook on his hand and sending the gun skidding across the concrete, stopping inches from my tire. Like a chubby Muhammad Ali who heard the ten-second bell, Alaguli unloads a barrage of lightning punches as I jump out and move toward the gun before my boy Kitch screams,

---

1   Son of. In this case: Ali, *son of* Imad.

"Fud! Don't ******* touch it!"

He knows I don't plan on using it, but he's wise enough to worry about evidence. On second thought, I agree. We form a wall in front of the gun, and the boys walk away. My heart races but I've already moved on from fearing for lost lives to basking in the drama. It's too early for a smile, but as I suppress it, I feel a smirk emerge, 'cause inside I'm ecstatic that I had a front-row seat to the best bout in '04, so far. Average days at Fordson fall someplace between rule bending and law breaking. But today was a better day: someplace between law breaking and lives lost.

اهلًا
My crew would stomp you
Leave you purple and blue
No, they ain't goons, but they looney
They truly go Looney Tunes
I'm looney, too, I write truly
And then go looney on tunes
Step to me, act unruly, I'll call Alaguli on you
The bully
My bodyguard, he need no 'toolie' dude
One punch: boom! Ha!
Now you in hospital room…

-*Looney Love, 2012*

I can only imagine what it felt like for Baba to inherit the case of Fordson High seven months later, midway through my senior year, when he stepped in as principal and began sorting through the files of his feelings—despair, disgust, disappointment, multiplying daily as he walked the halls of our district's largest public school, built with gorgeous bricks of granite atop fifteen acres facing Ford Road, Dearborn's main vein. It was America's first million-dollar high school, which more-than-doubled its accomplishment with a 2.2-million-dollar construction in 1928, the equivalent of over $40 million in 2024. But despite its beauty on the outside, Fordson functioned—at least for students—like a bankrupt prison on the inside: missing toilet paper in the bathrooms to symbolize the dirty politics; missing soap to unearth the stench of corruption.

I wondered how my father felt when he set German Shepherds loose in that same parking lot days into his job and uncovered enough weed in my boys' cars to supply a local dispensary. I remember what it felt like for me, at least.

> Class of '05, here we known:
> Druggies, dropouts
> Young dummies actin' grown
> Hard knocks, not lots

Of accomplishments to own

So, we let fights n' late nights set the tone

-*That 48, 2013*

It wasn't that we were much different than prior classes. We were just the tipping point. Explosive. The moment of eruption in a science experiment that mixed wretched schooling with bigotry and Islamophobia, as the ingredients of injustice bubbled in the basement of Fordson's history, slowly forming the perfect storm: the freshman class of 9/11/01. The class of a rising Arab majority. The class whom our White teachers and district leaders feared—and failed—more than any in Fordson's history.

Fordson, after all, was a microcosm of Dearborn, a city whose champion was a notorious White supremacist. A celebrated segregationist. A man who made his living by spewing mouthfuls of hate speech. "Some people, like the Syrians, are even worse than the ni**ers,"[2] he would say to cheering crowds on his mayoral campaign trail. He touted sloganeer promises to "Keep Dearborn Clean," understood by all to mean "Keep Dearborn White."[3] It required no decoding 'cause

---

2   "Statue of former Dearborn Mayor Orville Hubbard taken down." *Detroit Free Press*. Published June 5, 2020, by Niraj Warikoo. This infamous quote is published in other books and news sources.

3   Housed within the Henry Ford Museum collection is an ivory soap bar wrapped with an image of Hubbard's face alongside the slogan, "Keep Dearborn Clean With Hubbard Mayor." It appears that the product, produced by Procter & Gamble, was available for sale—or possibly distributed for free—between 1942 and 1978.

Orville Hubbard was haughty, and his hatemongering was hot off the press: "These [White] people [here] are so anti-colored...much more than you in Alabama,"[4] he bragged about his Dearborn residents.

His bigoted leadership kept him in power for nearly four decades best summarized by his nickname, "Dearborn's Dictator," given to him by critics yet celebrated by devotees.[5] Meanwhile, new generations of politicians and teachers carried the torch and traditions of Hubbard's agenda, one that explicitly called for the elimination of Black folk and an ever-growing population of "Syrians," the historical name referencing various Arab peoples who—combined with our Black neighbors—were deemed the "dirty" of Dearborn.[6]

Even in 1985, eight years after Hubbard left office and after Mayor O'Reilly Sr. had served two terms, their successor

---

4   Another infamous Hubbard quote in wide circulation across books and articles. It was first shared with the *Montgomery Advertiser*, a daily newspaper based in Montgomery, Alabama. Hubbard's overt racism is believed to have provoked the rise of the White Panther Party (WPP)—the White-ally group to the Black Panther Party, an organization dedicated to Black liberation. This history is detailed in a November 2021 *Penn Capital Star* article authored by Michael Coard, titled "The White Panthers: Genuine White Allies in the Fight Against Racism."

5   The Detroit Historical Society references Hubbard as the "Dictator of Dearborn," citing his notorious racism and his repeated reelection by over 70% of votes.

6   Under the Turkish Empire, Ottoman Syria (or Greater Syria) comprised of present-day Syria, Lebanon, Palestine, and Jordan. Egypt, most of Iraq, and part of Yemen were also under Ottoman rule. Westerners often referred to these collective Arab nations as "Syrian."

Mike Guido followed Hubbard's winning formula by distributing campaign flyers that urged voters to help him address "The Arab Problem."[7] Powered again by a spirited, anti-Arab base, Guido remained in power for twenty-one years, until his death in 2006. Meanwhile, a statue of Hubbard remained erect in our city as a symbol of White supremacy and "the ghost who still haunts Dearborn,"[8] until it was removed by his family amidst the Black Lives Matter protests of 2020. Still, his spirit survived, like an invisible hand that continues stirring the sentiments of anti-Arabism and Islamophobia that haunted—and still haunt—the halls of Fordson High.

And from when the Class of '05—now over 90% Arab and Muslim—arrived in 2001, until roughly four-out-of-five of us crossed the graduation stage four years later,[9] we were the unmistakable proof that Fordson was on the brink of collapse. It was as unmistakable as the planes that destroyed the Twin Towers during our first days as "Tiny Tractors." We were, in the eyes of our teachers, the not-too-distant cousins of the Mohammeds who made history in the worst manner on 9/11.

———————

7   "Decades after 'the Arab problem,' Muslim and Arab Americans are leading political change in Metro Detroit." *PBS NewsHour*. Published September 20, 2021.

8   The title of one *Detroit News* blog post that has since been removed: "Orville Hubbard – The ghost who still haunts Dearborn."

9   Fordson High's graduation rate was ~84% for the Class of '05, up from 80.1% for the Class of '04, according to Michigan.gov. The minimum threshold to meet Michigan's requirements for Adequate Yearly Progress was 80%. FHS also had a dropout rate of ~5%, meaning ~30 students in the Class of '05 alone dropped out.

The city of shawarmas, Mohammeds, Marwas
Arab immigrants who changed the ways it then was
When we first immigrated
We were awfully hated
Not to say *that's* changed
But to say the least, we made it!
Transformed the city in less than few decades
Now we're pushing escalades, publishin' essays:
Arabs in America: Persevere Hysteria
Move to neighbor areas
Seem to be afraid of 'ya
Treat Lebanese like disease
Valid reasons don't exist
Simply don't want you next door, Syria
Movin' out, movin' stereotypes about us
Cowards hit the Towers
Now it's: everybody doubt us
Teachers re-route us; so we stay home… irony
Now they keepin' tabs
On the money that we're wiring
Terrorist allegations, America's swamp of haters
Mouths open, teeth showing
I'll eat these alligators…
Khayeh I'll eat these alligators
                    -Sand Ni**ers, 2013

And, because they saw us as dangerous, as degenerates, the Class of '05 was collaterally damaged. Desperate.

Yet as we were evacuated from Fordson High and sent

home to our TVs, where we sat stunned as the Twin Towers burned and collapsed, and as the death toll at Ground Zero tallied toward 2,763 victims,[10] my class wasn't privy to many of our parents' insights; namely, that Dearborn and its surrounding towns would soon look upon Fordson's 2,500 students vindictively—each confirmed death deepening their hate for Islam, fueling their anti-Arab agenda, and promoting the idea that someone should pay the price for our nation's broken promise of safety. After all, who better to carry this burden than the boys and girls of Fordson High, the flagship school of America's most densely concentrated region of Arab Muslims beyond the Middle East?[11]

Within hours, as the "eye for an eye" climate grew, the eyes were increasingly on us. Within days, this heightened hate was evidenced by the constant bomb threats, including one that accompanied a box covered in tape and placed in the center of A-hall. Within weeks, this hate was heard in the hollers of hungry linemen before their quarterback's hike: "Sand ni**errr! Terroristtt! Towel headddd!"

Within years, this hate was headline news: Principal Imad

---

10   Death toll at The World Trade Center according to a 2022 figure. "September 11 Attacks." *History Channel,* A&E Television Networks, LLC.

11   The term "Middle East" was coined by the British Empire to refer to the middle of three regions under British rule. This middle region between the "Near East" and "Far East" encompassed the Arab nations of Southwest Asia and North Africa (SWANA). Although SWANA is preferred to the imperialist term, we use Middle East in this book for ease of understanding.

Fadlallah's school policies turned "Imposed Sharia [Law],"[12] Fordson High turned "Hezbollah High,"[13] Dearborn turned "Dearbornistan,"[14] a pair of FHS alums selling phones turned "Michigan men arrested on terror charges"[15] for "soliciting or providing for an act of terrorism"[16] by purchasing "prepaid cellphones that can be used to detonate bombs."[17] Even a decade later when Osama Bin Laden was captured and killed, Donna Spews, the same attorney and right-wing blogger who assigned these names to Fordson on her pseudo-popular blog—and who led an elaborate lawsuit against Principal Fadlallah that ended with the judge ridiculing her efforts—reflected on Bin Laden's killing with these words, in reference to Muslims:

"1 down, 1.8 billion to go."[18]

But when the late Dr. John Artis arrived as our new superintendent in the summer of 2002—just eleven months after

---

12   "Ex-principal, DPS sued by teacher." *Dearborn Press & Guide*. Published September 9, 2010, by Katie Hetrick.

13   "Arabs Behaving Badly." *Arab Detroit 9/11: Life in the Terror Decade*. Published 2011 by Nabeel Ahraham.

14   "Dearborn: Where Americans come to hate Muslims." *Bloomberg*. Published September 25, 2012, by Daniel Denvir.

15   "Michigan men arrested on terror charges." The Associated Press. *New York Times*. August 11, 2006.

16   An NBC News article published August 13, 2006, and sourced from the Associated Press, references these charges in connection to a similar case that occurred just three days later.

17   "U.S. Muslims say Midwest arrests built on profiling." *Chicago Tribune*.

18   Wikipedia.org. To avoid driving additional traffic to a blogger spewing hate speech, exact citations have been intentionally omitted.

that tragic September day—I couldn't see from his learned lenses what he began to see: a Fordson whose pretty face was a facade. I was a rising sophomore: shedding baby fat, soothing my freshman scars with suntan oil, shootin' hoops, trying to safeguard my smile and put one on my crush's face. Yet as weeks turned months, and months turned years, and our graduation neared, and as Dr. Artis kept fighting through the fog of one Fordson fiasco after another, it became clearer—at least from his frames—that Fordson wasn't far from Ground Zero.

So, from this desperate place, gripped by fear that Fordson would fall, and needing grace from God, John went searching for a "first responder" who could keep the lofty pillars on Fordson's front yard standing. And though he was new, Dr. Artis was a quick study, for he knew there was no better fit than Imad Fadlallah—the man whose very name means a *firm pillar* (Imad) by the *Grace of God* (Fadl-Allah), and who had saved one Dearborn Public School already, in a fashion that, Dr. Artis learned, was nothing short of heroic.

"No, thank you, John," was how Mr. Fadlallah demonstrated that firm grace.

But Baba could only fight it so much, 'cause his friend John was—foremost, and after all—his boss.

So, that's how Baba left Stout Middle School to become my principal for the second time.

Of course, that wasn't until the Class of '05 survived the rodeo of three and a half years without him. And we survived barely. For one, we were bad at the only thing that brought you any good at FHS: sports. It was our only saving grace before Fordson ever knew Principal Fadlallah. Football was the face-lifter for a failing school that faced the risk of state takeover.

And we were worse than bad. Following right behind two state championship-caliber teams, we were the worst Fordson football team in modern history. It was a hall-of-shame indictment. When our freshman football team finished 0-9, we only foreshadowed the embarrassment of our vilified varsity.

> Lost to Dearborn High, most our team high
> Coach pass by; never tell us "hi"
> Quick to tell us "bye" though; off to Ram's Horn
> After last game, we all there, where the fans go
> All the pretty ladies rarely caring if we lose
> We don't either, no *boohoos*, just "booooooo"
> -*That 48, 2013*

And so, the Class of '05 was chastised. Chuckled at. Counted-out. But celebrated or not, my quest was never in question, 'cause sports was all I knew. At least I wouldn't be like my brother Mahmoud ("Mac"), a senior during my freshman year who—unlike me—faced a difficult choice when he was a freshman: either be cool by playing football or be an outcast by caring about school. Well aware that Nerdland was a girl's world during those days, with few joys and fewer boys, he gave football a shot. And since he hated sweating, he figured, *I'll kick*. So, he visited the school library where Kicking the Football sat dusted on the shelf, and he kicked back to read it cover to cover.

That should've been clue enough, but it took a few missed kicks in his sweaty spikes before Mac realized he was a natural-born nerd. So, at first reluctantly and then with relentless pursuit, Mac dove in head-first: dominating debate tournaments and smashing spelling bees.

Yet even after he maintained a 4.0 and fought for months on end with the district to dually enroll in college, and even after he completed two years' worth of credits at Henry Ford Community College and the University of Michigan – Dearborn as a high-schooler—he was met with a rude awakening when he visited his counselor to request a letter of recommendation for U of M – Ann Arbor. She grabbed an application for a local college, pushed it across the desk to Mac, and said, "Here, hun, this is more realistic."

So, Mac began his journey at Albion College. But with his heart set on becoming a Wolverine, he kept his head down in the books and transferred to U of M – Ann Arbor one semester later—putting him on a path to become the then youngest partner in his law firm and one of the most sought-after attorneys in his field. And though his career came at the short-term cost of social suicide, it put him in long-term position to save himself—and later, to help save me—from the prison of minds.

PART I

PRISON OF MINDS

"Imad Fadlallah *saved* Fordson High School
and thereby saved Dearborn Public Schools."

-Trustee Mary Lane,
Dearborn Public Schools
Board Meeting, March 11, 2019

1. "WHO IN THE F*** ARE YOU?"

2002

We were gathered at an administrators meeting when my good friend and then superintendent of Dearborn Public Schools, Dr. John Artis, announced to the district principals: "I've hired Marshall Mills as the new principal of Fordson High."

When the meeting adjourned, I approached John. I was upset about the news, and I didn't hide it. I looked him square in the face and whispered loudly:

"John, you just made the *biggest* mistake of your career!"

Shocked, John replied: "What do you mean, Imad?"

"You've turned this process into a pissing contest, John! You hire the new kid on the block with no experience? You have no idea who this guy is or what he's capable of!"

I knew this was no way to speak to my superintendent, but I needed to make a statement. I was foremost a frustrated parent with a senior and freshman at Fordson High, alarmed by the revolving door of "acting principals" at the school.

With his face flushed red, John immediately shot back: "Our *process* is just fine, actually! Marshall was interviewed by three separate committees! He went through a rigorous

23

interview process and did a fine job! You don't know what the hell you're talking about, Imad!"

A fellow principal sensed the tension from a distance and quickly intervened: "Gentlemen, everything okay here?"

"Everything is fine, Doc," I said. "Just discussing the month's rent," I added, walking away.

John and I did not speak for months. In September 2003, I was attending an education conference hosted by the re- nowned turnaround principal Rick DuFour, a man whose work John and I were big fans of. During Rick's session, I received a call from my colleague Mike—a then administrator at Fordson High—and stepped out to take it.

"What's up, Mike?"

"Imad, I was told by the school accountant that Mills is stealing money."

"Is that all you know?"

"The accountant said she counted the cash from the foot- ball game and found a *lot* of money missing," Mike added.

"Who has access to the safe?"

"Just her and Mills."

"Does Mills know about this?" I asked.

"No."

"Mike, you need to call Mills and tell him the money is missing."

"But *he's* the one stealing the money!"

"That's none of your business, Mike. Report up to your supervisor and leave it alone. You don't want to get involved in this mess."

I knew the truth would soon emerge and wanted to spare Mike the drama of becoming too entangled. Mike phoned Mills and reported the news. Mills calmly assured, "Okay, I'll take care of it. Thank you."

But the school accountant took things into her own hands. She phoned the director of business services at DPS and made him aware of the situation. He hired a private investigator who reported to Fordson in early October and completed his duties before the end of the month. Mills had left a guilt trail a mile long. From asking a fellow administrator to drive him to a used car dealership where he purchased his daughter a ~$15,000 Mercedes Benz (which he parked at FHS so his wife wouldn't probe) to funding his drug addiction with money stolen from the Fordson football program, the evidence abounded. A deal was arranged that Mills wouldn't be fired and that the district would not press charges for the stolen money if he resigned. Like most scandals at Fordson and district-wide, the issue would be addressed in silence and swept under the rug.

And so, amid weekly episodes of false fire alarms and bomb threats, the door of acting principals at Fordson kept revolving, and chaos continued for two years until November 2004, when Dr. Artis paid me his second visit in two months at Stout Middle School where I had served as principal since 1997. John was a tall, wide man, at least six foot four inches, with a commanding presence. He entered my office with a concerned face and the same agenda as his last visit.

"Imad, I'm running out of options here. I need you to consider coming to Fordson."

"John, like I said, I have no desire to be there. I'm very happy here. I have a young family, John. I like the work-life balance I have. There are many capable administrators in our district who would love to make that move."

This time, I suggested a few names to John and provided a background on the individuals, hoping this would permanently divert the attention away from me. John was just in his third year of superintendency and did not know many of these potentially qualified candidates.

"Okay, Imad. Fair enough. I'll look into them," John agreed.

When John left, my secretary Dawn curiously asked, "Imad, what was that about?"

"Same story, Dawn. John wants me to move to Fordson."

"Well, what did you tell him?" she probed.

"No way! I'm not interested!" I said with a smile.

My smile was short-lived. A month had not passed before Dr. Artis was back at Stout on Friday, December 10, 2004, for a third and final visit. Being the courteous man he is, Dr. Artis never barged into my office, let alone into the back-office area. He always requested to see me and waited in the lobby for my secretary to summon me. But this time, he was already standing near my door, and when Dawn opened it, she had a very worried look on her face.

"Imad, Dr. Artis is back. This is it, Imad," Dawn wisely added.

Dawn was right. And this time, John did no asking. Just as his large frame filled the room, so too did his words: "Imad,

I am moving you to Fordson. I need you to do me this favor for six months until I can find you a replacement."

My eighth year as principal of Stout—where I had inherited a failing school filled with immigrants and refugees whose needs were unmet, and where students and staff united to become one of the highest-performing middle schools in the state of Michigan—would be cut short. Contractually, I understood that Dr. Artis had every right to do what he was doing. And on a more personal level, I sensed the urgency and fear in his tone.

"When John?"

"Monday."

"Oh *sh***," I blurted. "John, you know I would do anything for you… but will you bring me back to Stout?"

"I promise I will," John said, adding: "And if you want it in writing, you'll have it in writing. But just do me one favor, Imad: please, do *not* rock the boat."

"Your word is good as gold. I don't need it in writing. And I'll honor your ask—but I ask you a favor in return."

"What's that?"

"Do not label me 'acting principal.'"

"Why not?"

"Because I don't like to act, John. Imad Fadlallah is the new principal of Fordson High."

December 13, 2004, was a cold Monday morning in Dearborn, Michigan, and my first day on the job as Fordson's principal. I stepped out of my office sporting my favorite suit and tie and began roaming the hallways before third-hour dismissal at around 10 a.m. I felt lonely and flustered, partly due to the meeting held earlier that morning where Dr. Artis introduced me to Fordson's staff, who was less than welcoming. My mind raced with thoughts.

My position is a revolving door... the corruption is rampant... how will I approach this? Did I do all I can over the weekend to leave my Stout staff with all they need? There is consensus among teachers that cell phones and attendance are the two primary issues at Fordson—how true can that be? And who the heck decided to let kids leave Fordson's campus for lunch!?

But amid the doubts, a peaceful assurance loomed: *I'm only here for six months.*

Upon exiting the main office, I found a student in B-hall chatting on her cell, standing just feet from the main office entrance. I seized the opportunity to ensure that I was a good, new guardian of Fordson's building policies. Politely, I approached the student.

"Excuse me, you know that you should not be using your cell phone in the hallway during school time."

With a righteous tone and irritated expression, she turned and replied, "Who in *the f**** are you?"

Before I could react, she turned and began slowly walking away, apologizing to the person on the line and continuing her conversation. Shocked, I made a mental note of her face and varsity jacket and returned to my office. Within hours on the job, I was seated in my chair feeling defeated and asking myself: "Who in the F *am I?*"

I called my secretary Stacey into my office and shared the story.

"Don't feel bad, Imad. She really *doesn't* know who you are," she assured.

"Stacey, that is not the issue. I just can't believe students are speaking to adults in this manner."

Two days later, I held three consecutive assemblies in our school auditorium to reach all 2,500 students. After tracking down the young lady, Ayah, I asked my assistant principal to seat her in the front center of the auditorium. The assemblies were slight variations of one another. As I walked onto the stage, the students began to clap and cheer before I interrupted sternly:

"Don't clap! Don't clap! *Don't* clap!!! I'm here to introduce myself! My name is Imad Fadlallah! I am the new principal of this high school! The Dearborn Board of Education and Superintendent Dr. John Artis signed over the deed of this building to me. I now own this building! And *I am* the new sheriff in town!"

It was clear that in pretending to own the deed, and yelling like someone had cursed my mother, I owned the attention of the students. I shared the story of Ayah without calling her by name and capitalized on this teachable moment to address issues centered on language, respect, and values at Fordson High. It was a hard but meaningful lesson for Ayah. I stated that my early agenda would be to address academic achievement, behavior, and drug abuse. Lastly, I emphasized that we would come down hard on cell phones and tardiness to extend a hand of solidarity to the staff, though I had quickly learned these issues were far from priority.

Later that day, I transferred the highlights into a Power-Point and played the slideshow each morning, for two weeks, over the digital monitors positioned in every room at Fordson. I recall my son Ali, a senior at Fordson, coming home and relaying the experience to my wife and me: "You should've seen it, Mama." He laughed. "Every kid was frozen. After Baba spoke, I was the only one still smiling in the entire auditorium."

In reality, there was little to smile about at Fordson. Within days, I sensed the educational bankruptcy and soft bigotry that plagued our classrooms. After roaming the halls and talking one-on-one with teachers, counselors, admins, and janitors, I was disturbed. Students were the culprits in every conversation: "They're always tardy;" "They won't put away their cell phones;" "These kids fight too much, Imad;" "They're disrespectful;" "They don't want to learn."

When it wasn't the students, it was the parents who were to blame: "They don't know how to discipline;" "They don't show up to conferences or PTA meetings."

When I asked teachers how they hoped I would help, they made it explicitly clear that my job was to tend to their needs: "Well, how 'bout an air-conditioned room, Imad?;" "I need to be moved from the second floor;" "I need a math placement, science ain't workin' out;" "A parking spot closer to the door;" "A last-hour prep;" "Well, more money for supplies would be a start, Imad."

The list went on. But one implicit consensus seemed to emerge among the teachers at Fordson High: *Get rid of these students, and you will have a great school.*

Per Dr. Artis' request, I reported to Fordson less than seventy-two hours after the news that I had been reassigned. But just seventy-two hours after that, immediately following my "new sheriff in town" assemblies—as they were dubbed by staff and students—I phoned John and requested a meeting.

"Okay, we'll sit down after the PTA meeting tonight," John said.

After the meeting, John and I met in my office and had a heart-to-heart.

"John, I made a promise that I cannot keep. I cannot continue in this position without rocking the boat. I would greatly appreciate it if you will expedite the search and appoint a permanent principal as soon as possible."

"Why, Imad?"

"The staff here and I do not speak the same language, John. This building is at least ten years behind. All rules, policies, and procedures are designed to cater to staffers and not students. Kids are third-class citizens in this building."

John had a puzzled and worried expression. "Be specific with me. This is a lot of discovery for three days' time, Imad."

"Okay. Today I asked all eight counselors how many letters of recommendation they wrote for the graduating senior class. They *all* proudly answered, 'Zero.' When I asked about ACT prep, they explained that our kids don't need it because *if* they end up in college, they'll be down the street at Henry Ford Community College, which doesn't require an ACT. Our last graduating class of about 700 kids sent *one* child to the University of Michigan – Ann Arbor. And nine out of ten teachers don't see a problem with any of this. Instructional practices are mediocre at best, and in many classes non-existent.

"You want me to keep going? The teacher in charge of our school shop is $5,000 in debt to the school accountant and is making it up by selling our kids Red Bull and three melted chocolate chip cookies for breakfast each morning. My son Ali comes to school early just to buy that garbage. Kids are getting suspended by the dozens for not carrying an ID. John, this ship is sinking. There is a culture of soft bigotry and low expectations here. This is a prison… of young minds."

John's face was overcome with despair as if I had confirmed—or perhaps surpassed—his deepest fears. After a long exhale, he asked: "So, what is it exactly that you want to do?"

"Re-examine policies and procedures, and make the necessary changes to address the desperate needs of kids. This school is in cardiac arrest, and if we want it to breathe again, we need to immediately raise expectations, reduce the dropout rate, and open new doors of opportunity. We need to focus on the future of these children."

John looked me square in the face, and with a firm tone said: "Then go right on ahead. I'm with you."

"Thank you, John. But I should tell you now: if I start this, you will pay the price."

"I know that, Imad. That's a price I'll gladly pay."

"It is easier to turn a mountain into dust than to create love in a heart that is filled with hatred."

-Imam Ali ibn Abi Taleb (as)

2. PROM NIGHT

Amidst the chaos, senior prom was soon upon us, and my son Ali, a senior, was very adamant about reminding me: "Baba, do whatever you want here, but don't mess with our prom. I'm serious, Baba. Do *not* ruin prom."

As I stood inside the Hyatt Hotel venue, naive to prom culture, I watched disheartened as many of our girls walked in dressed in a manner that would've devastated their parents. I knew this because I was well acquainted with many of these parents, and I felt responsible for the heart failure they might've had if they were standing next to me to witness the events that transpired that night. It was common practice for many of the girls to leave their homes dressed in one manner only to change outfits afterward; but my concern over attire only revealed how naive I was, since drugs and alcohol traveled in the purses of these young girls to be shared with their dates upon entry. Within the hour, Fordson's students—many of them intoxicated—invaded the dance floor and practically mimicked a vulgar club scene.

I pledged that the Class of 2005 Prom would be the last one resembling a wild college party, so long as I was around. In 2006, I began "Prom Prep" early to manage teacher, student, and parent expectations. I warned that officers would be positioned at the doors and administering breathalyzer tests. Intoxicated students would not be allowed into prom. I also instituted a clear dancing directive: "Face to face; leave some space."

Students who did not comply with this directive would be asked to leave. As students began to share concerns that I was "ruining prom," a baseless rumor emerged that I was canceling prom altogether. Before it reached me, it broke the media—first, local news channels, and before long, CNN. Reporters visited Fordson High to interview students without permission: "How do you feel that your principal is canceling your senior prom?"[19]

I was stunned. Even more than a year later, in an article published online, Donna Spews wrote, "Imad Fadlallah has used Hezbollah High to impose his own personal sharia system, eliminating prom, harassing Christian teachers and coaches, and promoting Islam everywhere... I've written about how Fadlallah allegedly hit students. And I've also written about allegations that Fadlallah altered grades of Muslim students, allowing them to graduate, and graduated students with barely half the credits necessary to graduate [from] Dearbornistan Public Schools."[20]

---

19   This story was seemingly never aired or published by CNN or any legitimate news source. Nevertheless, Spews and others lacking integrity ran with this false narrative.

20   To avoid driving additional traffic to a blogger's pages spewing hate speech, exact citations have been intentionally omitted.

Later, Spews' false allegations went far beyond blogging, for it became item "21" in a document containing over seventy complaints and thirteen counts brought against me in a 2010 United States District Court lawsuit, where Spews represented her two plaintiffs pro-bono:

> "21. Fordson football players engaged in organized Islamic prayer before football games in violation of the United States Constitution's Establishment Clause and corresponding clauses under Michigan law and the Michigan Constitution, and Mr. Fadlallah canceled the school's prom dance because there was mixed dancing between males and females, and women wore sleeveless gowns, both of which he viewed as violations of Islamic law. The dance was eventually restored under public pressure, but conditions that complied with sharia (Islamic law) were put in place, regarding women's attire and other conditions. Recently, Fordson High School football team practices were moved to the middle of the night, in order to bow to Muslim Ramadan observance. On Election Day in November 2005, Defendant Fadlallah gave Fordson High School students who campaigned for Muslim and Arab candidates—[candidates who were] endorsed by the Muslim-dominated Arab American Political Action Committee (AAPAC) and [who were running] against Christian candidates for office in the City of Dearborn—the day

off from school, and extra credit to do so."[21]

One year after the case was filed—and months after my retirement—the court hearings kept coming, one after another, until the judge issued his final opinion: "This case began with highly alarming allegations of gross misconduct and nearly unimaginable religious intolerance manifested, most shockingly, by the highest-ranking officials in a public school. If it were true that a public school was being transformed into a religiously restricted, unconstitutionally discriminatory environment, and that objecting employees were made to suffer for their opposition to it, such information should have been proved up, and substantial penalties imposed upon the responsible parties."

The judge continued, "With the complaint, the fuse to this explosive case was lit. But it eventually fizzled out in the absence of evidence, or perhaps in the wake of inattention—the court knows not which. The court imagines that Plaintiffs could have brought a focused lawsuit that alleged a few (potentially) meritorious claims specifically tailored to the appropriate parties. Instead, Plaintiffs seem to have thrown at the Defendants everything but the kitchen sink—thirteen counts—in the apparent hope that one or two central claims might survive even without actual evidence. The strategy proved fatal. Most claims languished in want of discovery and

---

21   [Narcis] v. Imad Fadlallah, Case No. 10-13444 (E.D. Mich. Dec. 30, 2010).

remained undeveloped; the others were simply abandoned."[22]

Soon after the CNN interviews, I sent a letter home to parents explaining details related to senior prom. One topic that sparked a chain reaction from parents was my statement, "Prom ends at 11 p.m. Therefore, your child is your responsibility, and not the school's responsibility, after 11 p.m." My phone rang off the hook.

"What do you mean 11 p.m.?" parents asked. "My daughter told me that prom ends at 4 a.m.!"

The 2006 Senior Prom was held as scheduled, and the behavior was dramatically improved. I stood with a stick to signal that there should be enough room to place it between two dancing students and strictly enforced my "face to face; leave some space" policy. When the night ended, I came home, showered, crawled my exhausted body into bed, and told my wife, "I can't tell you how relieved I am that tonight's behind me."

But the 2006 Prom drama had just begun. When hundreds of copies of the school yearbook were released, one was delivered to my desk. I briefly skimmed the book before tending to my other tasks. Within the hour, a teacher approached, looking as if she had seen a ghost.

"Imad, I absolutely cannot believe they put that in the yearbook. I know you have to be outraged. That is *ridiculous!*"

I didn't have a clue what she was talking about. "Put what in there?"

---

22   [Narcis] v. Imad Fadlallah, Case No. 10-13444 (E.D. Mich. Dec. 30, 2010).

"You mean you *didn't see* the prom picture of you?" asked the teacher.

"Show me."

She flipped the pages to reveal what Ms. Spin, yearbook coordinator, had spun up this time: a photo of me with a stick and a caption that read, "Principal Imad Fadlallah enforcing Sharia Law at our high school prom."

I felt sick. There were cancers consuming the nervous system of our school building, and a new one had just revealed itself. There were signs, but no clear MRI revealing who and where each of these cancers were. I would have to learn on the fly.

Later that afternoon, I took the yearbook to the central office and showed it to Social Superintendent Mrs. Shrewd and the director of human resources. They appeared upset. Mrs. Shrewd promised that the matter would be appropriately dealt with.

After weeks of inaction and no follow-up, I paid them a second visit.

"Mrs. Shrewd, what happened with the Mary Spin situation? I am waiting on a word from you or Mark."

"I'm sorry, Imad. Mark is handling the matter. I promise you he will follow up shortly."

Mrs. Shrewd handed me my yearbook as if to say: *We won't be dealing with this. Let it go.*

In the end, not a single thing was done. Years later, Ms. Spin would be transferred to Edsel Ford High, where she was quietly fired for an incident that was brushed under the rug, right alongside the Mills scandal and dozens more within Dearborn Public Schools.

"Foolishness is the worst disease."

-Imam Ali ibn Abi Taleb (as)

3. THAT 48

That dearly held belief of mine—that the best days at Fordson are those that teeter between law breaking and lives lost—changed as soon as I became a victim of one. And during Senior Night at Ram's Horn, I manifested forty-eight hours of hell, beginning in a bathroom stall.

> In walks a past graduate, looked up to him
> But he threw me some bait of smack-talk, and I bit
> *-That 48, 2013*

Just as I turn around, Hani smacks me with all the force in him.

> I froze. Time froze; I'm thinkin', *uh-oooh*
> My mind left, *lek khayeh*, I even saw it go!
> *-That 48, 2013*

I stand frozen as he walks out. I call "Two" (Towfeek, *Allah yerhamo*[23]), one of the few recent grads I trust, and I'm yelling at the top of my lungs as I ask him to set up a fight between me and Hani at the park.

We're at Hemlock:

---

23 May God have mercy on his soul.

Swing for swing, pop for pop
Puts me in a headlock, *pah!* I finally drop
He's on top, Two stops it: "What you wanna do?"
"I ain't done, **** you!" Round 2:
Ding-ding, swing-swing, yeah I can fight
But I was no "ring king" that night, khayeh
Some said, "Draw." Others: "You lost it."
Don't think either cared, we're exhausted
                    -*That 48, 2013*

The next afternoon, my cousin Izzy and I are driving home
from the mall in the pouring rain, and we suffer a vicious
roll-over accident that should've killed us.

We're bumpin' Young Buck
And I'm crunk! I'm bouncin'
Gangsta life ain't fun—so how's it so arousing?
I'm chewin' on my mouthpiece
Izzy playin' Tetris
We bought our kicks, ate, kicked it for a second
Now on I-75, and it's pouring
Pourin' so hard at least a zillion worms swarming
Wipers goin' sniper fast; I'm goin' slow
Should be goin' slower though, like 30-below
Suddenly my front tire blow, then I lose control
Then time froze again, I'm thinkin' *uh-oooooh*
Are you serious?
My steering wheel is meaningless?
We're done; we're out

'Bout to be bloodier than periods
I said no prayer, nor yelled, "Life's a *****"
Shoot, I simply went mute
Izz did too; we hit the ditch
Then flip goes the Sport, flip again
Flip and half-flip
Three-and-a-half total, we live, God's grip

-That 48, 2013

I recorded and released "That 48"—a track from my *Dearborn* mixtape—eight years later as a twenty-five year old, from my bedroom in my parents' home just two blocks from Fordson. It's my story of forty-eight hours, a capsule of my childhood: the drama, the trauma, the boyhood joys, the mischief, the misguidance. And in many ways, it's a capsule of the Class of '05 and Dearborn at large.

'Cause something felt eerily familiar about that City of Troy police officer who made the ambulance wait as he wrote up a ticket and fought through the windy, torrential storm to knock on the truck's big red doors—where I lay waiting on the other side to be rushed to the hospital—just to hand me a ticket. He wasn't at the scene of the accident, yet decided anyway that I was guilty of reckless driving in severe weather.

It wasn't just the punishment that felt familiar. It was his cold demeanor. His apathy for an injured Arab boy on a stretcher, with a funny last name and too much blood in his mouth to explain himself. I knew this officer because he was—all but literally—my football coach. He was my basket-ball coach. He was my teacher. He was my principal—that is, whenever Baba wasn't.

> Cop hands me a ticket to top it off
> As if it wasn't enough, I got Sergi Federov'd
>   -*That 48, 2013*

Lying there on that stretcher felt just like weeks prior, too, when I was lying on the locker room floor about two minutes after Coach Stern—my varsity football coach—asked me, "Son, why you are still standing here? With your gear on?"

Hesitating, I confessed, "It's my birthday, Coach. The boys are waiting to jump me."

I felt shame for avoiding it, for being a "sissy." But Stern and I both knew this wasn't the brotherly kind of birthday beating, 'cause I had a target on me. The kid with the big house. The full basketball court. Stout Middle School boy. Principal's son.

And Stern knew this as well as I did—partly 'cause he targeted me, too.

In fact, by then, both Stern and I had caught wind that the price on my head was put there by none other than Ali E, our thick and hairy running back, who looked twenty-three in ninth grade, and whose signature move was charging head-first like a bull into the belly of linebackers before bursting forward over their laid out bodies for long sprints into the end-zone, where he often lifted his helmet to vomit, then smile—his own kind of touchdown dance. And who, on that day, stood in his still breath like a patient predator behind God-knew-which-wall-or-locker in that giant maze of a locker room. E had recently published his latest "hit list" on loose-leaf paper one morning in the cafeteria where students congregated. Hundreds ate their free cereal or eggs, but E was hungry for something else; and for weeks, if not months, his hit list was the talk of our class, especially since he wasn't one to not deliver on his threats.

Everyone wanted to be the first to let me know that I was E's next linebacker, so to speak. There were even a couple girls on E's list, which only added a layer of crazy to his already-secured legacy. It was a long, fluid list, too—in pencil, but precise—with people moving in and out of the hit list lineup, sometimes before or after a beat-down, and I kept a hard face at every update. But my heart would drop to my gut each time I learned I was still penciled in, abs tightening for the blows that could come at any moment I was caught slippin' or alone.

And for the Class of '05, no subject matter or sheet of loose leaf at Fordson captivated our imagination, carried our attention, and inspired our discussion like the one that came from the spiraled notebook of E, a bully who soon became my brother. But not before the beat-down.

So, looking up at the City of Troy police officer from my stretcher wasn't much different than looking up at Coach from the ground, two minutes after he replied to my birthday line with, "Well, we gotta get home, son," letting a slight smirk emerge as he kept walking, as if not only to say, *I'm not getting involved*, but also, *good luck, sissy.*

The stench of his silent shaming as he walked away was like a shot of steroids. With a puffed chest and arms flexed, I strolled into the locker room, where I went one-on-ten with the Lowrey boys (featuring some Woodworth bandwagons) as the crew threw me to the ground, unloading on my body like a dummy bag before E began counting his vicious blows up to seventeen, as I braced my body in new places between punches, relying on both skill-work and guesswork like a soccer goalie in a penalty situation, until seconds after "seventeen" came, when Coach appeared to lazily say, "A'ight… knock it off," before walking off again.

Lying on that stretcher was much like the feeling I had almost one year after those forty-eight hours, too, on a particular night when three years of peer pressure and the early onset of a deep depression took their toll, and I was hoping to smoke weed for the first time. More so, I was hoping it lived up to its hype. By then, I had graduated into a "grade 13" situation, a freshman at U of M – Dearborn but practically still a Fordson boy, except with some reality checks: submitting a final paper that my brother wrote and getting caught (that nerd had it published online); failing that course; finessing Bs and Cs in my others, and losing my friend Ahmad tragically when he was attempting motorcycle tricks in a parking lot.

And on this night, while parked in the abandoned motel behind Andiamo, Izzy and I were caught and thrown against the Tahoe where the cop cuffed our wrists. Some of the boys argued the miracle was that I was still a sober kid. Others argued the miracle was how dumb we were to leave East Dearborn to park on the west side, especially when Detroit was a shorter drive away, *and* get caught, let alone on my first try. Not that the two miracles are at odds.

But we and the Dearborn cops often were, and since I dared to say "yes,"[24] the officer seemed quite pissed off when I dared to plead with him, too: "Sir, please, just let me call Officer Joe! He'll tell you I'm a good kid!"

"Shut the **** up!" he screamed as he shoved me against the passenger window and tightened the cuffs until they caught my skin and crushed my wrists, ignoring my shriek as he led me to his car and shoved me headfirst into that dark, backseat pit of torn, dirty black leather.

> First night I tried to blaze, I got arrested
> Izzy rolled the blizzy, I kicked back and rested
> Told the cop I know a cop
> He grabbed the cuffs and pressed it
> Tighter... "Aghhw! **** man!"
> Bigot, yup, you guessed it
> *-Blueberry Mary, 2013*

And yet, lying in that stretcher with the ticket in hand was just the icing on a burnt cake, 'cause so much more captivates me when I reflect on "That 48." Like the irony of my mouth getting me in that nasty fistfight the night before it crashed into my steering wheel, helping me break the wheel in half—right

---

24   A reference to the common slogan "Dare to Say No," which was part of the nationally funded Drug Abuse Resistance Education (D.A.R.E.) Campaign. D.A.R.E. programs were inspired by the "war on drugs" and enforced by local police departments, especially in the 1980s and 1990s. Ironically, t-shirts and other merch that read "D.A.R.E. *To Keep Kids Off Drugs*" became popular in drug culture.

after I recited every word of G Unit's "Beg for Mercy" mixtape, religiously in sync with every syllable, pausing on a lyric only to chew on my mouthpiece, a habit from football season that I held onto like my dying hopes of stardom, now reduced to repeating after rap stars, tasting the malice of their lyrics on my lips at every twist and turn in my Ford Explorer Sport Trac.

> Young Buck still spits, as I bleed
> The truck's in pieces, so are my teeth
> Bye bye, sweet smile
> My crown count is three (plus three)
>   -*That 48, 2013*

And when the tire blew, and the Sport Trac slid off track into a ditch, and my life flipped upside down, and all around me was being bent and destroyed, and my unbelted body floated mid-air before bouncing around like pinball, and I lacked wisdom to "beg for mercy" then, Allah (swt) spared me anyway.

The only part of me that was seriously damaged was my mouth—the thing I had *really* lost control of by that point.

> Anyway khayeh, the other day I'm reflecting
> On all the times that I wisely used
> My mouth to protect me
> And then all the other times
> My mouth got me into deep
> And how it took seven years
> Of visits to fix my teeth
> And how those 48 hours
> Of being a coward changed my life

And how when you keep going down
The wrong path you get signs
And how mighty, mighty powerful
The mouth really is
And how we should watch it
Same way we babysit kids
'Cause the pen—the mouth—is
Mightier than sword
So let's not praise our ego, khayeh
Let's praise the Lord

-That 48, 2013

And of course, there was Two, who saw me for who I was—partly thanks to the bond he had with my aunt Rima, a then teacher at his Lowrey Middle School alma mater. Two overlooked the rich-boy reputation that I couldn't seem to shake off and took me under his wing; and when I called him to set up that fight with Hani, I knew he'd force it and be a fair referee. Though I lost the fight, I had won respect for taking on a former starting lineman, who was two years my elder, especially with Two as our ref.

But Two was more than a protector. He embodied my hopes and dreams. A six-foot-four inch, 270-lb. football star—All West honors, doer among dreamers, gentle giant among boys, and able to do what I (and most) could only dream of: command Coach's respect, inspire his conversation, even bring out his stingy smile and lethargic laugh.

So even when, at U of M's football camp the summer before my junior year, Two filled my pop with Pepto-Bismol, rubbed Icy Hot all over my body during my sleep, and stuck my hand in a glass of warm water so I'd pee my pants after hours of diarrhea—I was embarrassed, but I only pretended to resent him for it, 'cause I still couldn't see him as anything but a hometown hero, and secretly felt a bit honored to be the source of his entertainment. Because soon, I knew, Two would be gone, college-bound and bound to do better than me and most Tractors, and I could proudly decorate his college bleachers with a blue hoodie reppin' Grand Valley State where he had committed to play. But like many of our childhood friends, he would never live to get there. And like many-a-Dearborn death, we were left to mourn not only our brother's absence but also the elusive mystery behind its cause.

"The best kind of *jihad* is to speak a word of truth to a cruel king."

-*Prophet Muhammad (s)*

4. BROKEN

As happy as I was for the Towfeeks in our town, I—like most Fordson boys—dreamt of being on that college field for myself. An entire childhood's worth of high hopes awaited on the mountaintop of Fordson football and basketball, a mountain I climbed while towing a steel training sled strapped to my shoulders, welded by Baba in Fordson's metal shop one Saturday while he was Stout's principal. I wonder if it was nostalgic for him, revisiting the room where his career began as a metal shop instructor at Fordson. Or was, perhaps, the nostalgia clogged by a sense that something had gone seriously wrong in this building since his time here? I wonder if he had the thought, even for a fleeting moment, that he would one day be called upon to save Fordson High. Whatever his thoughts were, I know they gathered into those beads of sweat that always collected on his forehead, droplets of determination that probably dripped into the steel that he melded into a pole, secured into the center of my sled, before he dropped a forty-five pound weight around its circumference, and gifted it to me so I could run—like Forrest Gump—through trophies and accolades, year after year: Offensive MVP for freshman basketball, Overall MVP for JV basketball, Overall MVP at

Next Level Football Camp in Inkster, Offseason Dedication and George B. Lewis Memorial Awards for varsity football, Jack Castignola Award at the University of Michigan's football camp in Ann Arbor.

But once I finally reached this great mountaintop of Fordson varsity sports, I found that the adage "hard work pays off" was far messier when politics or playing favorites were involved. For although I might've been an attractive target for our quarterback and Coach Stern—who we all knew loved to win football games—perhaps I was also an attractive target to help Coach win political wars, especially keeping Arabs (and Fadlallahs) in their place, anywhere beneath the positions reserved for the powers that be. For the time being, Baba was still busy steering his ship at Stout Middle School, but perhaps whispers of the many attempts to recruit him to Fordson High had reached Stern—whose watchful eye saw Imad Fadlallah gaining influence in the community. Perhaps seeing another Fadlallah—Baba's cousin—already in administration at Fordson, rubbed Coach the wrong way, and he felt that he had to choose which game he wanted to win more. Or perhaps he was simply playing favorites, a status that I could never seem to gain with Stern. No matter how liked I was by other coaches or teachers, my accomplishments and positive reputation elsewhere meant nothing to me; 'cause it was Coach Stern who stood between me and my dreams.

And it was this, more than anything else at Fordson High, that broke me: the unexplainable pain of a dream deferred. The invisible abuse of adults with elusive eyes, refusing to acknowledge you. The silent sneers that make the void of love grow loud in your mind—crippling your confidence; sabotaging your self-esteem; gaslighting you blind; seducing you into submission. This was the reality of how I—and many—were raised year-round, for four years, across Fordson's fields, courts, and classrooms.

But years before that, I was still a short, chubby kid who wasn't sure puberty was promised, waddling through the seventh-grade hallway at Stout Middle School and anticipating the full force *sahsoohs*[25] that lasted a few months until I punched Omar in his face. I kept unloading on him until Mr. Mashhour locked his arms under my pits and yanked me off.

I was no fighter, though. I was the principal's son who feared Baba and at least one of my bullies. As much as it ate my pride alive, and angered me, I preferred Omar and Muneer's *sahsoohs* each morning over Baba's wrath if I were suspended, or worse, getting jumped if I snitched. Status quo seemed like my only option until my *amto*[26] Rima read my distraught face one day and made me fess up, grabbing me by my shirt with all the Fordson alumna in her.

"You listen to me, and you listen carefully: the *next, time,*

---

25 Neck slaps.

26 Aunt (paternal).

he smacks you, *if* you don't turn around and kick his a**... I'm kicking *your* a**! Do you understand me!?!"

"What about Baba! He'll kill m—!"

"I don't give a sh**! If you don't kick his a**, I'm kicking yours! *Do* I make myself *clear!?*"

My lips quivered at the thought as I uttered, "Yeah."

Before long, I had taken on both of my school bullies and served one out-of-school and one in-school suspension, including the three days when Baba led me and Muneer into the scorching sun, handing us each a heavy shovel after he traced a large circle in the dirt and said, "dig," before marching off, leaving us digging and dumbfounded, with no apparent goal or destination in mind.

So, things were lookin' up when I looked up from my locker one day, after the bully sagas, to find JR excitedly telling me about the nation's largest football camp at U of M.

"If my parents say 'Yeah,' I'm in!" I exclaimed.

"Well, it's only for high schoolers," he added, killing my hopes.

"Huh?! Then why the hell did you tell me about it, bro?"

"Well, I'm going to write a letter asking for an exception."

"Oh... okay." *Who thinks of that? That must be from his White side*, I thought.

The camp staff wrote back and invited us to be the young-est—and perhaps first ever—incoming eighth graders to attend camp alongside the nation's most elite high school ballers. When day one arrived and JR's grandpa pulled up my drive-way, I was standing in my sweats and sporting my silky "Ali" boxer-briefs—designed to look like Muhammad Ali's fight shorts—that Mama let me buy from TJ Maxx. It was my perfect way of containing my pre-puberty excitement—I was The Champ already.

But Mr. Jimmy John's—by way of a foot-long tuna sub—had other plans for me. By the time they measured our heights, weights, and my pathetic vertical (I'm not even sure I left the ground), JR and I had been separated into the sea of student-athletes on the floor of U of M's Track and Field gymnasium, when suddenly, my stomach was speaking six or seven foreign languages I had never heard—yet fully understood.

At first, I knew it was getting bad, but after evaluating the ~2,000 legs I would have to walk over, all while defensive coordinator Jim Herrmann spoke on the high stage above us, I decided I should wait and not be responsible for giving eighth graders a bad rep. By the time I realized it was an emergency, I also realized—in a mortifying fashion—that food poisoning could cause paralysis and that "makin' a run for it" was officially ruled out.

I'm not sure which of the memories hurt worse: the way the boys beside me began slowly distancing themselves, forming a circle around my reeking body as I squirmed in a puddle of my sweat and feces; or the way some of them started to cover their noses with their tank-tops. Or was it the way one of them swung his arm up and down like a dramatic windshield wiper, which almost gave me the power to move because I was dying to break his nose for him, just to help him out? Or the way the staff carried me onto the golf cart to the bathroom—the only bit of grace being that Coach Hermann finished talking and the group was dismissed, giving our cart room to move? Or when one of the trainers handed me a new pair of oversized Hanes undies and told me to throw my boxers away (I started to ask if he thought there was any hope for my Ali briefs, but I wizened up and bit my tongue)? Or the following day, when I was standing in a line of 100+ boys at our breakfast buffet with JR, and like a scene out of a sitcom, a camper pointed at me and hollered, "Dude, aren't you the kid who *sh*** his pants yesterday!?" as several others erupted into laughter?

So, I felt especially fresh when, four years later, as a rising senior, I became the real camp champ, sitting there on the same gymnasium floor and being shocked out of my skin when head coach Lloyd Carr began speaking about a stu-dent-athlete from Fordson, a *four*-time camp attendee, and one of the top receivers at camp with a 4.3 GPA who had just finished third place in the "best hands competition," where I caught ball-after-ball at increasing miles per hour from the football-throwing "Jugs" machine.

"There is nobody more deserving of our camp's most prestigious honor," he said.

It was the Jack Castignola Award for Outstanding Stu-dent-Athlete, awarded to one athlete each year and named in honor of a legendary football coach who was known, among other things, for his mottos like, "You must be willing to pay the price."

I had paid mine, except there was one problem: when Coach Stern pulled me aside just a couple hours before Coach

Carr presented me the award, he asked, "Son, don't you have a four-point-somethin'?"

"Overall? It's probably a high 3.8 now, Coach."

"You don't have a four-point somethin'?!" he shot back, annoyed.

"Last semester I did, Coach, a 4.3."

"4.3. Okay. Okay." He nodded. "Listen, I'm goin' to nominate you for the Jack Castignola Award. You have a real shot."

"Thank you, Coach."

He walked away on a mission. The whole interaction left me confused. There was something transactional and distant about his demeanor; Coach pulling me aside for a one-to-one chat was unprecedented enough, let alone nominating me for the Jack Castignola Award. After not even congratulating me for earning the bronze medal in the best hands competition? And never saying hi or giving me face? Is he having a change of heart? And is he about to lie about my cumulative GPA, which the award is partly based on?

When I heard Coach Carr read off my list of accomplishments, including my "4.3 GPA," I felt somewhat deserving, yet also fraudulent. Even from my naive place, I wondered if somehow, this gesture from Stern—who also got his nods of public recognition from Coach Carr during my award speech—might be more self-serving than anything else. And soon after, my suspicions were confirmed in the most dream-crushing manner.

Nevertheless, with my enormous trophy towering over my collection of others at home, it was beginning to seem like my hard work—the 7 a.m. off-season mornings when I trespassed over Fordson's fence to run bleachers, the training sled work that brought my forty-yard dash down from a fat-boy 5.2 to a respectable 4.7 seconds, or the long-distance track I ran to bring my mile down to five minutes while pissing off all my other football teammates who I crushed during conditioning—was all cashing in at the perfect moment.

Weeks later, Next Level Football Camp at Inkster High only confirmed my potential, and the camp director, a former D-1 linebacker himself, awarded me the camp's overall MVP:

"Ali... what can I say? This young man did it all this camp, and yesterday when he was lined up at corner, he had the nerve to tell me 'Watch this pick-6,' and then actually delivered on that same play!"

But as he and other coaches congratulated me, asking where I planned to play college football, I was embarrassed by the bizarreness of the whole scene. It seemed to me like I had succeeded in manipulating a whole staff into seeing me as better than I actually was. 'Cause by then, I was convinced that I was dispensable. Average, at best. Sure, I had made a summer splash, but I didn't even seem to be on the radar of my high school coaches, especially Stern, let alone *a college*.

We left camp for Fordson's weight room, and that day I was afraid to tell Coach I had won MVP, even fearing it may discredit the Next Level staff, whom I admired. So I stayed quiet and hoped Coach wouldn't ask. It was no surprise when he didn't, until he turned to AK, our star running back.

"How'd you do, son?" Coach asked.

"I won Offensive MVP, Coach." AK replied.

"That's great, son! Congratulations! Anyone else win anything?"

"Yeah, Fadlallah was Camp MVP!"

My stomach knotted, awaiting confrontation.

"Are you serious? *Fadlallah* won Camp MVP?" Coach interrogated AK some more before walking over to me. "Son, you won *MVP*?"

"Yes, sir." I replied.

"Well hell, why didn't you tell me?"

"I don't know, Coach."

"Well, that's great, son!" he said, slapping me on the back before walking away. I was nervous and ecstatic, all at once.

Then came summer ball, 7 on 7, my chance to prove that the camps weren't a fluke. All summer I didn't drop a single ball, including an outstretched, one-handed catch in the endzone on a slant route for a touchdown that drew *ooos* from the crowd and a smile from my offensive coordinator, though it almost seemed Coach Stern didn't notice. Meanwhile, he would walk in step with our QB, or running back, or linebacker, with his arm around them as he let them in on his state championship-winning wisdom.

He *definitely* noticed that one-handed catch I made on a 4-route about twenty minutes later, though, because after the defensive back grabbed my right arm, threw his left forearm into my ribs, and ripped my entire cutoff before the ball arrived, I managed to reel it in with my left arm before getting in his face and signaling for a first down. It was a violent pass interference, and when I saw Coach sprinting toward me, I was certain it was to congratulate me for containing the ball and my cool. *My day has arrived, baby!* I thought. Instead, he grabbed my face mask with both hands and yanked me toward him before he began cussing me out, letting me know, "You'll never play another ******* down for me if you ever get in a defender's face again!"

I never dared to. And perhaps that's what earned me two play calls in game two of the season: one 3rd down out-route that I caught on the sideline for a big first down, and the second in crunch time when I bobbled and dropped a pass that would have put us in position to win. Maybe that drop gave Coach permission to do what he had planned to do all along: never throw me the ball again for the rest of the season, except once, during our very last game.

> You saw my potential, turned a blind eye
> Looked up to you, trusted you
> Gave love to you… why?
> Abusing your power; abusing emotions
> You put me on the field, then you put me in motion
> Audibles on audibles you called on my life
> I called for the ball
> That's when you called for the knife
> Straight in my back, until I say "I can't breathe!"
> Never asked for this, got Kaepernick'd
> Down on one knee, like:
> Tell the truth; tell the truth; tell the truth
> 'Cause now I know; now I know; now I know

My father is why; Coach, how did he threaten you?
I know you knew better, still it would get to you
Took it out on me; you saw the scout on me
Didn't let me shine; you casted doubt on me
Robbed me my chance; robbed me my dream
Even buried it, but God turned your scheme to a seed,
see...
I don't talk about it; I don't blog about it
They don't know what we know
I often thought about it...
How you did all this damage, but I got nothin' to show
We don't tell one another, but we all know
And when you showed to his funeral looking humbled
I could tell that you had stumbled, and you fumbled
I think you're probably a better man today
You don't have to be the man who ran away
From the truth...
I still love you, Coach; I used to hate myself for it
Because if only you knew the hell I gave myself for it
I shamed me, blamed me, for all I was victim to
Today I wonder *maybe*, you regret a thing or two?
It's never too late to know the truth
   - 2017, Untitled, Unreleased

Slowly, Coach turned his back on our entire team, and the Class of '05 reputation recreated itself anew: players skipping practice or showing up high. A few, like Bous, even quit mid-practice to stick it to Coach.

"Boussy, where the *hell* do you think you're goin', son?"

"I quit! *Coach!*"

Stern sat us down in the gym for one last time after Senior Night.

"Now, if anybody feels I did them wrong, if anybody feels they got somethin' to say, well stand up and say it now. Nobody? *Nobody* wants to say somethin'?"

Sitting there with my helmet on to hide me from reality and the only heartbreak that hurt worse than the one my ex-girlfriend gave me, I still believed Coach was somehow unaware of his wrongdoing. I thought perhaps it wasn't personal. Perhaps it was more about giving up on the Class of '05. I still admired him and wished he would take a chance on me, a chance that had expired football-wise, but not relationship-wise. I had still never entertained the idea that I was targeted. I was just a wide receiver wishing I *was* targeted.

How could I have known that my father was an emerging threat to the existing power structure and status quo within Dearborn Public Schools? How could I have foreseen that just weeks later, Baba would be Coach Stern's new boss—and that during the first game of my senior basketball season, Mr. Fadlallah would have to get in Stern's face and put him in his place?

For now, I was just trying to process the shock of Coach's words as they reverberated off the gym walls, echoing on repeat in my mind: "Nobody wants to say somethin'? *Nobody* wants to say somethin'?" Heartbreak fueled my adrenaline as my desire grew, a desire to let Coach know he did me wrong, and perhaps to gain the love that young kids seek from their coaches—love I had seen Coach give others, never in large doses, but enough-so that I knew he was capable of it. With courage mustered from my naive heart, I stood up and began speaking through quivering lips, telling him I was robbed of a fair shot. But as soon as I began, one of the assistant coaches—Coach Berro—yelled at me like his job depended on safeguarding the secrets of corruption that I was now interrogating:

"Shut *your mouth* and sit *down!*"

For a second, I considered complying. But I recalled two years prior when Berro, whom I loved and admired and who was previously my basketball coach, forced me to apologize to an opposing team after one of its players told the referee I whispered, "A bomb is waiting for you on your bus" in between free throws. It was the most uncreative of unoriginal lies when you're playing Fordson; and although Berro knew this, he insisted I apologize. I argued with him until he gave me an ultimatum: "Walk over to them and say sorry or *say bye* to the 4th quarter!" So, I pled guilty. But I learned my lesson then, and I wouldn't betray myself again.

"Why?" I protested. "Coach Stern asked us to speak. I'm not being disrespectful or sayin' anything wrong."

"No, no, it's fine. Let him say it," Coach Stern said.

I continued, "Name me a player who worked harder, Coach. I deserved the ball this year."

"He's right," my teammate Hemi interjected as he stood up. He then followed my words with a plea of his own, both in my defense and his.

Coach Stern gave in a little, acknowledging that we did work very hard and that "Maybe I failed you as a team." In the moment, his half-hearted admission was a perfect pacifier, a nice cooling balm on our open wounds. *Maybe I'm not crazy* was almost all I wanted my thoughts to whisper after months of questioning my sanity.

The anger served me well on that same gym floor weeks later, in our varsity basketball season opener, when I took the fury of our football failures out on Inkster High with a 21-point, 12-rebound game that earned me nods in the next day's newspaper (which I wouldn't have known about if not for JR, who was then a student at Edsel Ford High and who read the newspaper each morning before school. Five years later and I was still thinkin', *Man I love that boy... that must be from his White side!)*

Despite my performance, I wasn't the main headline from that night since a nasty brawl broke out during the game, and Coach Stern, now athletic director, involved the cops against the orders of my father—who was now his boss. By the time Baba was done confronting Stern, Stern realized the "new sheriff in town" meant business when he made it clear he wasn't there to act. And on that day, Baba made it clear that he wasn't there to play, either.

But in my mind, I was *only* at Fordson to play. And though my varsity basketball coach, Coach Locke, was a kinder man, he too would barely acknowledge me after my great game—or ever, for that matter.

So, *his* father, Coach Locke Sr., a Fordson legacy, approached me the day after the Inkster game with an agenda I could intuitively sense. "Hey, Ali, impressive performance last night, kid, but—"

"I know, Coach. It won't happen again."

My face flushed red from my own words, which shocked us both. It was as if, from that nervous place of yearning for acceptance, I blurted exactly what I sensed he wanted me to believe. And, ironically, it was as if he felt a bit defeated by my submission, knowing I had not spoken with a rebellious spirit, but rather in the spirit of laying my season's destiny in his hands, to be shaped as he and his son wished.

Perhaps his conscience pricked over how much I trusted him and how easy it would be to slay my dreams. And so, still startled, this older man, whose heart was humbler but still tainted, and who had coached my beloved aunt at Fordson— the same aunt who made me take on the bully, and whose number 30 jersey I wore in both sports in her honor, and who I watched swish her way through four seasons on varsity where she earned college scholarships, and who also coached me into the clutch-shooter I was, too, and whom Coach Locke Sr. bluntly told, "Laura will score her 18-20 points. Martha will score her 16. Then, you can score…"—had returned a whole generation later, arriving just in time for my breakout game, to deliver me the same blow: "Well yeah, uh, well, no, it's not that, Ali. It's just that this team was playing street ball, son, you know, and it's not always going to be that easy for you."

I got the message—at least in the naive way I was supposed to—and I fell in line, becoming the role player with minimal ball time I was coached to be. Despite strong scoring games, leading the team in rebounds, and coming up clutch in big moments, I became dispensable again, barely scratching the surface of my potential.

So, after dropping off my helmet to Coach Stern months earlier, and hitting the ditch where my truck flipped three times, and now, after dropping off my basketball uniform to Coach Locke, I began speeding downhill into darkness, with two seasons of utter disappointment in my rearview, past prom night when I half-heartedly entertained my new date as I was still trying to process the (second) heartbreak my ex-girlfriend delivered to me, just days before.

Weeks after prom, it was past midnight and we were rollin' two cars deep into the Ford Road Sunoco, our ski masks stuffed in our hoodies or pant pockets as a dozen of us walked inside to buy a dozen eggs each. We had seen enough law enforcement from our school librarian, watching one victim after another fall prey to his policing of school policies as he stood outside the library door each day, disapproval emanating from his aura as he seemed determined to ensure the books would stay dusted in our absence.

In over 700 school days at Fordson, I had never seen a smile on Dr. Halloway's face, and tonight, as we made the fifteen-minute trip to his home, I was determined to keep it that way. My heart raced as we parked two blocks away and began the long walk toward his wide ranch, a confident swag in our step like the cops were in on it, our ski masks on like Grand Theft Auto. When we approached, our boy Baz gave the orders that we launch at "Ready, aim, fire!"

But Baz couldn't get halfway through "Ready?" before Bous rifled the first two eggs straight at Halloway's window from forty feet (typical Bous), its explosive sound and mile-long echo shocking me far more than its splatter. Those two minutes were at least two hours in my mind as I vacillated between delight over what a disaster Halloway's house was, and anxiety over what a disaster *my* house would be if Baba caught wind. But we were never caught.

It was a perfect contrast to almost four years prior, during my freshman year at Fordson, when the Lowrey boys (and the same Woodworth bandwagons)—led by none other than Alaguli—let a few dozen eggs loose on *my* house, just 'cause.

"You don't know who did it?" Baba probed.

"No."

"You have *no* idea?"

"Probably Alaguli and his boys."

"Why?"

"I don't know. About a week ago Alaguli told me, 'I'm gonna egg your house.' I didn't do anything to them. They've hated me since before I even got to Fordson. They tried to jump me at the Lowrey track meet last year—before I ever met 'em. I don't even know how they knew me."

"Okay."

Within hours, Baba had the name of each egger and had somehow summoned all of them to our home. Minutes before they arrived, Baba called me down: "Sit on the porch and wait for them."

This is a terrible idea, Baba, I thought. *This isn't how you make Fordson boys resolve s***. This is only gonna make 'em hate me more. I'm gonna get jumped 'cause of you!*

But just like the boys, I had underestimated the savvy of our soon-to-be principal.

"Boys, have a seat. How are you guys?"

After engaging them in pleasantries for a few minutes, which only made all of us more nervous, Baba turned to me. "Ali, what are you doin'? Go grab your guests something to drink, and some snacks."

A minute later, I was pouring pink lemonade into red cups, handing the boys small paper plates, and letting them pick between the crunchy blue or soft red Chips Ahoy! cookies (Alaguli grabbed plenty of each). As they sat there, eating, as confused as me, Baba walked over to the garage, returned with a large yellow sponge, grabbed the hose, and began hosing the house down, cleaning the countless eggs off the face of our home.

One of the boys jumped out of his seat. "Mr. Fadlallah, let me help!"

"Sit down," Baba commanded. "Ali, come clean," he added.

I had no idea what his strategy was—at least then—but I knew it was working. Baba knew the boys assumed I saw myself as "superior," perhaps because of our home, or apparent income, or Baba's influence, or all the above. Baba knew I didn't see myself in this manner, but he also knew that only by humbling me in front of the boys—and doing the same himself—could that image be undone. And that was how Baba—time and again—turned his vandalizers into vanguards who saw him as a father figure, and who championed his causes.

But for the time being, there were very few causes at Fordson for me and the boys to champion, other than becoming teammates and brothers—first in sports, and now, nearly four years later, on the streets, as we vandalized Dr. Halloway's home.

And for the first time as Fordson Tractors, we looked forward to visiting the library, each of us eager to read Halloway's face and leave him with a smile. We would soon thereafter cement victory by setting a dozen chickens loose in the hallway for our senior prank, right in front of the library's doors. Halloway was livid, and it seemed the Class of '05 had the last laugh.

Six years later, while serving in the Teach for America Corps in Clarksdale, Mississippi, I received an email from Baba asking me to edit a eulogy he would be delivering the next day. When I downloaded and opened the doc, I was shocked: it was for Halloway. As I read over the words, the shock only intensified. *This is Halloway?! Caring about kids? Married to a Palestinian? The guy hated us!* A wave of guilt rushed in like chickens coming home to roost, my resentment evaporating with the realization that hate, however seemingly righteous, was a horrible emotion to harp on.

And so, as I polished Baba's beautiful speech with a few minor edits, I began to replay our years with Halloway and re-examine my preconceived notions. There was no doubt about Halloway's disdain, evidenced by daily stares of disapproval, despite not knowing us. But perhaps Dr. Halloway, who earned his PhD from U of M, was demoralized because he knew how far the divide was between us and those books. Perhaps he felt we were too illiterate—too far gone—to see their value, and thus, his value. Perhaps he was even a different Halloway with the 1% of Fordson kids who visited the library willingly. Regardless, I *know* he was a different man when Baba arrived. So perhaps Halloway had just about given up on us until Mr. Fadlallah restored love, hope, and discipline in the same hallways Halloway once patrolled.

In the eulogy, Baba would open with a light-hearted story:

> "One day I called [James] and said, '[James], I got a call from the superintendent asking me about a sign posted in the library saying, 'Have you embraced Islam today?' Do you know anything about such a sign?'
> He responded, 'Well, Imad, for the past nine years, the closest thing to religion anywhere near the library were the worry beads I placed in Abe Lincoln's hand.'
> He was referring to the statue of Abraham Lincoln at the entrance of the library.
> [James] got me out of so many jams. At least once a

month, someone or a group of visitors or alumni visited the high school. Part of the tour was the library... and it never failed: someone asks a question about a mural on the wall, or a statue somewhere in the library, or what kind of wood was used to build the chairs, or the fireplace. And [James] managed to read my facial expressions, and right away he knew I had no idea what the answer was. Politely and diplomatically, he chimes in with an answer that covers every corner and requires no further questioning.

I had the honor and privilege to serve with [James] on many committees. He was precise and concise: 'Tell me exactly what needs to be done, and I will get it done.' I remember when [one student], Abbas, wrote the winning essay for the Dr. Martin Luther King Jr. Scholarship contest. [James] printed the essay and posted it in the showcase by the library, as well as on the school's website. As if his own son had written the essay, [James] was glowing with pride for the student. During the budget cuts, we had to move [James] to the classroom to teach English. I was very worried about such a change—moving someone from the vastness of the library to the confinement of a classroom. He loved the change, and he embraced it. He told me that he could not believe how much fun he was having.

At one of the committee meetings, a teacher hijacked the conversation and kept dwelling on the same issue for several minutes. As an administrator, I kept my cool, while making several failed attempts to correct course. [James] did not waste time. Very openly, he told the teacher: 'You already said x, y, z, and you've been repeating it for ten minutes. Can we move on? I have kids waiting in the library.'

I knew [James] the librarian, I knew [James] the historian, and I knew [James] the teacher. But most of all, I knew [James] the human. Every time he returned from Palestine after his short vacation, and left Reema behind, I felt his heart, I felt his emotions, I felt his beliefs, I felt his love, and I felt his passion for justice, equality, human rights, and especially for the children of Palestine. On behalf of every staff member you have worked with, on behalf of every student you have touched, we love you, [James]."

And so, I—along with the Class of '05—began to reap what we sowed as we rode our Tractor into graduation and beyond, unaware that our seed-drill had become contaminated, and that our four years of harvest would bear us few good fruit.

I graduated and entered "Grade 13," a year of depression and dependence, until I had dug for myself a desperate hole at U of M – Dearborn, both emotionally and academically, and lay in it, defeated.

And it was from this hole that my cell rang "Mac" for

probably the 60th time in 100 days, and I answered expecting his familiar refrain to enter my right ear and exit left: "Ali, you should leave Dearborn. I don't care where you go but if you come here, I'll help you transfer to the University of Minnesota. You need a new start."

This time, less because I saw the promise in my brother's words, and more because it was the only thing left that I *hadn't* tried, I said, "Okay." And slowly, but surely, my life would change. But first, I had to make it out.

We took up a half-row in the Star Theatres at Fairlane Mall and were just halfway through the previews before security approached.

"Y'all gotta leave. *Now.*"

We knew Mahdi had a history with security, and a probation record that meant another fight would get him locked up, but we also knew he was a much calmer and more collected version of himself. So even when three security guards began escorting us out with grim faces and no stated reason, Mahdi wasn't looking for any trouble, and we weren't expecting any. In fact, I was afraid of the thought when at least eight to ten more guards accompanied the trio, forming an army behind us. I could see we were clearly outnumbered, and it would be ugly, and I'd either have to fight hard or lose all my cred with the boys. But all appeared under control—until one guard, perhaps feeling emboldened by the rare compliance of these Fordson boys, decided to shove Mahdi in the back just as we neared the exit doors.

Within seconds, it was an all-out brawl between us and security, right on the front property of the theatre. We made our own movie that night, blood spilling on the concrete as we each took two at a time, before sprinting to our cars and flying off the radars of Dearborn Police whose sirens colored our rearview mirrors as we sped off just in time.

But this time, victory came with no regrets. 'Cause for once, Mahdi didn't start it—he was just forced to finish. In fact, Mahdi was reforming before our eyes—beginning his path back to Allah (swt), to being guided by *Rasul Allah* (s)[27] and our Holy *Imams* (as),[28] and to being freed from his mental prison. *Shaytaan*[29] was making desperate attempts to seduce him back, but Mahdi was a new man—a transformation that helped plant the seed that one day, I too, could make that change. Though not before I served my time—seemingly a life sentence—in the prison of *my own* mind.

---

27   The literal translation is Prophet of God, though *Rasul Allah* is commonly used specifically for Prophet Muhammad (s). The "s" stands for *sallAllahu alayhi wa alihi wasallam:* may God grant His blessings and peace upon the Holy Prophet and his Progeny.

28   Holy Imams refers to the twelve successors of Prophet Muhammad (s) who possess divine knowledge and authority, and who are among the 14 Infallibles of Islam (the other two being Prophet Muhammad, s.a.w.s., and his daughter Fatima Al-Zahra, a.s.). The (as) stands for *alayhi salam:* peace be upon her (or him).

29   Satan.

"Indeed, your good deeds toward the enemies and jealous ones who scheme against you are more irritating to them than if you were to take an offensive stance. And it is also a motivation for their reform."

-Imam Ali ibn Abi Taleb (as)

5. "HEZBOLLAH HIGH"

One March afternoon in 2005, three stormy months into my first year as principal and days after my forty-fifth birthday, Dr. Artis paid me a visit at Fordson High, waiting in the lobby like he did at Stout to be escorted into my office.

"Good morning, Imad. Good to see you."

"Good to see you, John. What's going on?"

"Well, you've been here for three months now, Imad. I'm wondering if you've given this any thought?"

"Given what thought?" I asked, suspecting John was referring to staying at Fordson, but still hopeful that I was mistaken.

"Have you considered staying?"

A suffocating feeling overcame me. I knew my career had taken a permanent shift, and John and I both knew I didn't have a choice; though this time, it was not because he was forcing my hand. Rather, it was because it became obvious that when former director of human resources at DPS—Karl Steuff—began his relentless efforts to recruit me to Fordson in 1998, even to the point of pestering my wife, his words were resoundingly true: "Fordson High needs a major makeover."

"I knew you would do this to me, John."

"You know we need you, Imad. These kids need you. And

I truly thank you."

I barely had time to process the news before Dr. Kassem, English teacher at Fordson and one of the angels of hope in our building, paid me a visit.

"Hi, Imad. I've asked Mrs. Swan for a copy of the AP scores, and she hasn't delivered on her promise. Can you track those down for me, please?"

"Sure."

I emailed Mrs. Swan right then and requested that the test scores be given to Dr. Kassem. Mrs. Swan replied stating that she would send them over shortly. I didn't revisit the matter, and Dr. Kassem didn't either, until the following year:

"Imad, I asked you for these scores last year and you forgot about me. I want my scores," said Dr. Kassem.

I felt guilty, and promptly called Mrs. Swan. "Mrs. Swan, I want this year's and last year's AP scores on my desk, and I want them now."

When the scores arrived, I handed them to Dr. Kassem. Later that afternoon, she returned to my office.

"What's going on?" I asked.

"I thought you may be curious to know why Mrs. Swan was reluctant to share the scores last year," said Dr. Kassem.

I opened the test results. Over 85% of students in the other English and language arts course, taught by one of Mrs. Swan's closest friends, failed the AP exam. Conversely, roughly 90% of Dr. Kassem's students consistently passed the AP exam with a score of a 4/5 or 5/5.

This story represents the factions that were characteristic

of Fordson High. Often, these factions were formed across lines of race and religion. One such example involved a confrontation between Mr. Fence and Dr. Kassem—who sponsored the National Honor Society and supported her students' wishes to host a fundraiser for the children of Gaza. Mr. Fence, a teacher whom I had recruited to join me from Stout, was torn between his loyalty to me and our kids, and his loyalty to new friends who assembled my enemy faction at Fordson. One day, he stormed into Dr. Kassem's room, scolding her for promoting religion on school grounds. The controversy at hand was that the students had prepared chocolates for the Gaza fundraiser with a wrapper that included this saying from Prophet Muhammad (s): "The ink of a scholar is more sacred than the blood of a martyr."

Dr. Kassem wasn't one to back down. She shot back at Mr. Fence, perhaps questioning whether he would object to quotes about being "a good Samaritan"—a Biblical reference—or even one that wished us a Merry *Christ*mas. She reminded Fence that being a Prophet of God does not disqualify one from being a historical figure, or a quotable one, for that matter; and most importantly, that it was within the rights of students—and thus, none of his *or her* business—whether they decided to use the Prophet's words to promote their secular and humane cause.

Meanwhile, the 100% student-run and volunteer-driven event, which came under constant scrutiny from within the building and beyond—including from the Board of Education—would raise over $60,000 for Gaza. At the event, Dr.

Robert Simon, founder and chairman of the International Medical Corps, said, "I have attended hundreds of fundraisers worldwide. This is not only the most organized fundraiser I have *ever* attended—but also the *only* one entirely run by students. I am beyond impressed."

The opposing factions at Fordson were also fueled by conflicting ideologies about what students were capable of. This reality is captured in no story better than Abed's, who was on the list of chronically absent students who I called into my office each year, with hopes of rectifying the issue. Somehow, Abed had twenty-four absences in each of his classes except third hour, where his absence count was just *three*. At first, I suspected Abed may be enrolled in a class like those of my son Ali's former "cool" teachers, who didn't care to mark absences or tardies. But when I realized his teacher was Dr. Kassem—who I knew wouldn't let this slide—I was puzzled.

"Hi Abed, have a seat, please. Is your third hour teacher not marking you absent?"

"No, she does. I only missed three days when I was in the hospital. I never miss third hour."

"You only missed three days of third hour, but twenty-four days of every other class?"

"Yes sir, Mr. Fadlallah."

"Why are you only showing up to third hour?"

"Because…uh, wallah, I don't know, Mr. Fadlallah."

"Yes you do."

"You won't understand." Abed said, nervously.

"Try me. I really want to understand."

"Because that's Dr. Kassem's class."

"I can see that. So what?"

"Dr. Kassem is different. She makes you *think*."

Abed's words were a slap in the face, only affirming what I already knew about the culture of low expectations that pervaded our classrooms. I had to keep a straight face and hold Abed accountable for his absences, but the truth was, I just wanted to embrace him. Like many encounters with students who forced me to examine the lack of engagement they were victim to, it was Abed who was holding *me* accountable.

These conflicting ideologies concerning student potential became a constant tension that caused Ms. Dalilah, my assistant principal, to sneer at me during a professional development presentation, when I said, "*All* children in our building, regardless of their background, can and will learn." She was offended by this notion and turned to her friends—teachers at Fordson—to criticize my statement aloud: "yeah, *right*."

Early one morning during our first days of school in late 2005— the beginning of my first full year as principal—I walked out of my office into a rowdy line of over 300 students. I turned to Ms. Dalilah and asked, "Why are they in line?"

"Because they don't have an ID."

"Why are they coming in for their IDs now?" I asked.

"Because they cannot get into class without an ID. That's our building policy."

"How long does this process take?"

"Two to three minutes per student."

"Two to three minutes per student," I repeated, nodding my head in disbelief. "So, the last student in line could lose over 900 minutes of instructional time?"

Ms. Dalilah looked annoyed and puzzled as if she did not understand why this matter was even in question.

"Well, if you look at it that way Imad, I suppose, yes," she said.

"Okay. Please do me a favor, Ms. Dalilah. Go to your office and send out a building email that we no longer require an ID to get into class."

Ms. Dalilah stared at me as if I had lost my mind.

"I *can't* do that," she said, matter-of-factly.

"Why not?"

"Like I *said*, Imad, it's a building policy!"

"I understand, Ms. Dalilah. And I just *changed* the policy. Please send the email out as soon as possible."

Shocked, Ms. Dalilah left and sent out the email. Mayhem ensued. Within days, teachers began remixing the ID policy, suddenly requiring IDs to take tests or to participate in a field trip. Teachers struggled to sacrifice this power play. The ID rule was leveraged to send students to the office or, almost as often, home. Fordson was the only school in our district—and the only school I knew at all—that required an ID. Hundreds of instructional hours were lost to this ineffective policy. Worse yet, the ID rule—or the expectation that our inmates should "show their number" at all times—was just one of dozens that created a prison-like climate.

A couple weeks after I had changed the policy, I called history teacher Mitch Morgan into my office.

"Please have a seat, Mr. Morgan. Why are you requiring students to have their ID in class when I gave a clear directive to cease this policy?"

"This is my rule, Imad. It has always been a rule that I strictly enforce."

"Listen, Mitch, the difference between you and me is like the difference between the federal law and the state law. In this building, I have to be the federal law, and your state law should not contradict mine.

"If it does, you're stepping all over me, Mitch, and we cannot have that here. We gotta be on the same page."

Mr. Morgan was upset, but he got the message. Before he left, I added, "Mitch, there will be some changes here. I understand that many of these policies were instituted under the umbrella of teaching kids responsibility. That's a good idea, and some aren't bad policies in theory. But when they are implemented at the expense of our students' education, we are failing our children. We deviate from the goal. We send them home, and they lose learning for the day. We can't afford that."

Mitch looked skeptical but gave me a nod. "Understood."

Whereas Fordson High resembled a prison for students, it was a lawless land for teachers, who sat isolated on their private islands. They were wardens of their classroom. They decided what rules to implement and what instruction—if any—would be delivered.

Many teachers, for example, took it upon themselves to create a policy of locking their doors immediately after the bell rang. Tardy students would not be permitted to enter the classroom. This, the teachers claimed, was a great way to teach students promptness. But the teachers neglected two key facts: first, school safety regulation policies prohibited locking the doors while students were in the classroom, so their tactic was illegal;[30] and second, students were frequently tardy for legitimate reasons—a request from their previous teacher, a summoning from the office, a medical issue, a field trip, et cetera.

Shortly after the ID fiasco, I issued a directive requiring teachers to keep their doors unlocked at all times unless they were leaving their classroom, and no children were inside. A handful of teachers refused to follow this directive, too, claiming that they were afraid for their safety. This was, in fact, true. Many teachers at Fordson High *did* fear our students. Locking their doors gave them a sense of security that, like the IDs, they could not imagine sacrificing. A couple of teachers insisted I would have to write them up before I could expect them to comply.

Even in my fourth year as principal, Mr. Price, in particular, would not budge at any cost:

---

30   Amidst increased school shootings and related safety concerns, new laws were introduced, and the door-locking policy has been modified by many schools/districts. In many cases, including within DPS, teachers are now permitted to lock their doors when students are present. Still, most districts stipulate that this should be done only in times of imminent danger or emergency.

"I will not unlock my door," he insisted, "no matter who gives the directive! Be it Fadlallah or Whiston![31] I will die on top of the hill!"

Weeks later, I spent my morning in a hearing with Mr. Price as we sat before union representation. His demeanor transformed entirely. "I have no issue complying with Mr. Fadlallah's directive and will do so from here forward."

"And your claim that you will 'die on top of the hill,' Mr. Price, and not follow this directive, neither from me nor from Superintendent Whiston. Did you not say that?" I asked.

"Yes, I did."

"So, what has changed?"

"Well, I just got married. I bought a house. I'm in a better place right now."

Yet incidents related to IDs and door-locking policies paled in comparison to the countless other crises and covert operations taking place at Fordson High. In 2005, I was notified of two horrifying cases in which students were victim to physical and sexual assault at the hands of Fordson wrestling coaches. Right after I sent Coach Ivan home, a letter was left in my mailbox. It accused me of targeting and firing the preachers in our

---

31   The late Brian Whiston, who succeeded the late Dr. John Artis as superintendent of Dearborn Public Schools.

building, among other religiously motivated acts of injustice. When I read it, I suspected the voice was that of Mrs. Wendy Wix, an English teacher who wrote me many emails in her distinct tone. I called her into my office.

"Wendy, did you write this?" I asked.

"Well, I *signed* it," she replied, rebelliously.

"I know. That's not what I'm asking. Did you write this?"

"I *signed* it, like *everyone else.*"

"That's not what I'm asking, Wendy. I want to know if you wrote this letter."

"Why do you think I did?"

"Because reading between the lines, this sounds like your writing."

"Yes, I wrote it."

"Okay, Wendy. Why would you accuse me of anti-Christianity practices?"

"Because you fired the *first* preacher, then the *second* preacher. Seems to *me* like you're after preachers!"

"Wendy, the first preacher, Coach Bark, took a Muslim child to Port Huron one Sunday afternoon, without parental permission, and had one of his children force his head underwater at their lake home while his daughter snapped pictures as he yelled, 'Hallelujah, now you're a Christian!' Weeks later, Coach Bark threatened to release the pictures on the internet if the boy denied being baptized. Bark confessed to this boy's allegations.

"The second preacher, Coach Ivan, took a couple of students to his home for a sleepover and sexually molested them.

This was a matter of criminal investigation. Now, it just so happens they're preachers, Wendy, but there's nothing I can do about that.

"Also, you should understand how this business works. I don't have the power to fire a teacher. I reported these crimes. I did my job. The district investigated the allegations, found them to be true, and *they* fired the preachers."

Wendy's mouth dropped. She was deeply apologetic.

I ripped the letter in front of her, adding, "You know what, Wendy? Tell your friends that I will pretend like this never happened. And please relay the message that just a little bit of trust will go a long way."

As Wendy walked away, I sighed a deep exhale and stared down at my desk where the handwritten testimony sat, prepared by Haroon, when he detailed the case of Coach Bark's assault:

> "Coach [Bark] told me about this camp… and I said yes. A week later, I gave him $265 cash, but the coach said no, I already paid for you. The camp was 3–4 weeks away. I asked [Rudy], [Bark's] son, what we [were] going to do there, and [he] said, 'The same thing our family does every time: play Frisbee, football, swim, volleyball, swim again, eat, and go home.' I said, 'Okay.'
>
> When we arrived there, [Bark] started telling me all these stories about people converting and told me, 'This is why I came to Dearborn: to make some common sense to you Arabs that you should follow Jesus.' I specifically told him, 'What I am going to do is stay

Muslim.' When I told him, 'No,' I would not convert, he got mad later on, because he would not talk to me.

He made us form a circle. [Coach Bark] said, 'Introduce yourselves, and tell all of us how Jesus came into your life.' When it was the Lebanese woman's turn, she introduced herself, and these are the exact words she said: 'Many of you know me, and I am guessing you know my whole family are Christians except me, but now I am converting today because when I was Muslim, I used to read the Quran, and every time one of them would try to make me read the Bible, I would say no and throw it aside. I used to sell them in garage sales. But then every night I would realize that the Quran didn't make any sense to me and gave me no signs. [Then] I run into [Mrs. Bark], and she told me to come to church with them and see if I would like it, and I really did, so I threw the Quran aside and sold it in my last garage sale and also took off my scarf. When I started to read the Bible, I think God answered me and my prayers, and that took a month. But the Quran didn't make sense at all, and after seven years of reading the Quran and wearing the scarf, nothing made sense.'

After she was done, we left to the water. [Bark] started being nice to me, and I just went with the flow and [assumed he] probably understood me [well] and will not force me to convert. Then all of a sudden, he looks at his son and stared him down and went to whisper to him about something, and all I heard [Rudy] say is 'No, Dad.' [Bark replied]: 'Just do it, [Rudy]. He won't do a thing!' 'Em, ok.' Then [Rudy] came to me from behind and suplexed me (flipped me, a wrestling move) into the water. His dad came running and picked me up from underwater and yelled, 'YEEHA!' and rubbed his hand on my head and looked toward his daughter and his niece and raised my hand in the air very high and smiled at them, [all] while I was trying to rub the water off my face to see what he was doing.

About two months pass, we started school, and one of the Fakhouris came and asked me, 'Hey, [Haroon], is it true? Did you convert?' and I said, 'No, why? Who told you [that]?' 'Oh, [Mr. Bark] showed us pictures of you in the water getting baptized.' I said, 'No… why you asking me this?' He said, 'Oh, because if you did convert, I was going to call people and jump you.'

After two weeks, more people came and tried to jump me [at the] gym lockers during gym time or while I was on my way to class, and I'm not going to lie to you, this is my first time being afraid of fighting, not because I'm weak and I'm afraid, [but] because I want to graduate and go to college.

In conclusion, [Bark] set me up so he can tell the other wrestlers, 'Look, your friend converted; why don't you convert?' And now all I am thinking about is that [Bark] is at his house laughing with his family and saying, 'Bam, we caught a sucker!' But it's okay with me because I don't talk to the wrestlers anymore because they wouldn't defend me in the first place. Also [Mr. Bark] can say or think that I am one of them and I am a Christian, but to my other friends, family, [Bark's] son, and me, I am not 100% Muslim but 200% Muslim, whether [Bark] likes it or not.

I wrote this because I don't want anybody that joined Fordson's wrestling team or anybody else [to go] through what I went through these past few months and also [to] warn them to not fall for [Bark's] tricks."

Signed,

[Haroon]

I was overcome with a feeling of despair as I re-read Haroon's testimony and wondered how much fear he must have carried with him, how his parents felt, and how many more Haroons roamed the halls of Fordson High wearing scars given to them by school staff who were supposedly there to safeguard them. Fordson, I kept learning, truly was a maximum-security prison where staffers were protected at all costs, and inmates were given the bare minimum needed to survive.

Worse yet, the Barks in our building were being praised for their work not only on the wrestling mats, but also on the "pulpit" of our prison halls. Coach Bark, the Alabama-bred missionary and former Auburn football player, was deemed a hero. In the December 2002 edition of the Christian publication *Charisma Magazine*, Bark was lauded as the "Detroit Soul-Winner" for his success in "Reaching Muslims in America's most Islamic City," as the subtitle of his feature read.

In the article, Coach Bark shared a story of a nightmare in which he was chased by a vampire, a terror that awoke him and left him searching his Bible for answers before calling out to the Lord for help:

> "The Lord let me know this was the spirit of Islam. It was here to scare and intimidate people so they will leave the Muslims alone. I think the Lord put me through that to let me see the reality of this thing."

In another 2003 publication by *Ministries Today*, after Bark was nominated as an "Innovative Risk-Taker" and praised for his work on "behalf" of Muslim children, Bark added the following:

> "You've got to reach past and touch people. If you don't, they'll stay foreign to you your whole life. And you're going to miss a world of opportunity for the Lord to teach you. That's not fun. That's called regrets at the end of your life."

The reality was, he led a ring that resorted to manipulation and molestation as part of its prison ministry service—on more than one account. And it became evident that his fellow coach and closest companion took Bark's words of "touching others" quite literally.

So, in response to the "constructive" criticism—even among my supporters—that I tried to "clean house" too aggressively and too quickly, I reiterate here for the record what I told one young teacher: if I have *any* regret, it is not being a bigger bully to the criminals in our building. I regret not coming down even harder, even faster, on those who were committing crimes at the expense of our vulnerable children.

"And remember when those who disbelieved plotted against you to restrain you, or kill you, or evict you? But they plan, and Allah plans. And Allah is the best of planners."

-The Holy Quran, 8:29-30

6. ASSASSINATION ATTEMPTS

I could not have foreseen the onslaught of attacks that would ensue, nor their magnitude, as I began holding employees accountable for their gruesome acts. Soon, I would be required to provide my first of countless testimonies to the district and court of law. As I sat down to write, I began with the case of Haroon:

> "...[Mr. Bark] did not deny any of the student's accusations except for making the threat. [He] insisted that what he does on Sunday is none of my business. I tried to reason with him and explain that the ninth grader is on his wrestling team, and [thus], he cannot use his position as a coach to proselytize students. Also, [the student] is a minor, and [Bark] should have informed the student's parents. Reasoning with [Mr. Bark] was impossible; therefore, I thanked him for his services and banned him from coaching.
>
> A few months after, [Mr. Stern] walked into my office to tell me that a teacher in my building, [Coach Ivan], was arrested over the weekend [for alleged sexual assault]. I called [Mr. Ivan] down to the office and

asked if the rumor was true. His response was, 'Based upon the advice of my attorney, I cannot discuss this matter.' I asked [Ivan] for a yes or no answer. He kept repeating the same response.

I called the head of the youth bureau in Dearborn and asked her to run a search for any police reports. No report was filed in Dearborn. I was very worried since [Mr. Ivan] indirectly confirmed the rumor. I looked in the [district employee directory] and realized that [Mr. Ivan] resided in Melvindale.

My secretary Stacey also resided there. I asked her if she knew anyone in the police department. She said, 'Well, I know the chief; I used to babysit his kids.' She called the police chief, and [he] told her that I should call Lieutenant Hayse. Lieutenant Hayse gave me a copy of a police report filed *by* [Mr. Bark] against [Mr. Ivan]—his fellow coach—for improper sexual conduct against one of the victims at Fordson.

It was almost 1:30 p.m., and school dismissal was at 2:15. I called the superintendent and the director of human resources and informed them of my findings. The HR director asked me to call [Mr. Ivan] down to the office and tell him that he will be suspended with pay, pending the outcome of the investigation. Needless to say, [Bark] and [Ivan] were both friends and preachers at the Assembly of God, and the brutal reality at the time was my inability to explain to the staff why I suspended 'the second preacher.'

Melvindale Police were investigating based upon an accusation by [Bark]. When I called [Bark] again, he was not cooperative at all, and insisted, 'You should leave this matter to the Almighty—He will take care of it.'

He also told the student [victim] not to speak to me about this matter. The next morning, I visited the mother of the other student who was molested [and informed] her of the situation. I sat around her kitchen table while choosing my words carefully to minimize the shock. The mother was dumbfounded; she explained how [Bark] and [Ivan] were frequently in her home playing Monopoly with the kids and how much she trusted them both.

The following morning, Lieutenant Hayse paid me a visit and wanted to interview the victims... Afterward, I interviewed one victim to conduct my own internal investigation. It was one of the most challenging tasks I have ever performed in my career. The student had built a thick wall to block everything off. [But] one crucial piece of information was confirmed...

I called the lieutenant and asked if the student mentioned that his pajamas were wet. The lieutenant did not know. Melvindale Police picked up the pajamas and sent them to the state police crime lab for DNA analysis. On Friday, December 16, 2005, at 8:30 a.m., Lieutenant Hayse and Assistant Wayne County Prosecutor Dan Less walked into the main office [and requested] me. I recognized [Mr. Less] immediately since I was the jury's foreman on one of his cases a couple years prior, when Mr. Less thanked me for 'making his case'—a similar one to the case he was investigating now.

Mr. Less and Lieutenant Hayse informed me very apologetically that they would be dropping the [Ivan] case for lack of evidence. I was stunned to hear they may very well allow a sexual predator to work with children again. 'What about the pajamas?' I asked. The lieutenant responded that although the DNA on the boy's pajama matched the DNA of the accused, the accused could always claim a wet dream.

I stood up, trying very hard to contain my disappointment, and asked them both if they had some time. They responded yes. I called the student down into my office after calling his mom and informing her of my plan. I explained to the student the situation we were in and the purpose of the visit by these men in my office. I told him that this matter is in his hands, and that he needed to share every detail of the truth with the lieutenant. [Then], I walked out.

Two hours later, Mr. Less and Lieutenant Hayse opened my office door. Both shook my hand firmly and thanked me. Hayse said, 'Thank you very much; you are in the wrong business. You have made my case.'

I have not and will not reveal what the student shared with me [and the lieutenant]. Throughout this ordeal, my first and utmost priority was to protect the identity of the students. But I can tell you this: I firmly believe that had I not gotten that student's testimony, [Ivan] would still be in a local building, teaching today."

Prominent members of the church community—who were upset and suspicious of my intentions—reached out to request a meeting. After we sat down and I put these cases in proper context, the clergymen were much more reasonable in their approach. Before long, the many articles accusing me of firing preachers were replaced with articles that unearthed the truth, albeit many months later. In February 2006, for example, just fourteen months into my new role, the *Detroit News* published the following article (shortened for brevity):

> MELVINDALE -- A Dearborn Fordson High School coach and teacher faces a preliminary hearing [on] Feb. 13 on charges that he molested two students.
>
> Melvindale resident [Ike Ivan], 46, is a youth pastor at the Assembly of God Church in Dearborn and a wrestling coach at the school, police said.
>
> He was charged with two counts of criminal sexual conduct and released Tuesday on a $50,000 cash bond, police said.

"The juveniles involved were on either or both of those (Fordson) teams," said Melvindale Police Lt. Chad Hayse. "The juveniles spent the night (at Ivan's house). There was inappropriate touching involved. He is not to be back at Fordson school events or near any schoolchildren."

The incident occurred over Labor Day weekend, when Ivan invited the two boys to his home in the Northpointe Townhomes in Melvindale, police said. They slept in the same bed, and [Ivan] fondled them, police said. One of the boys told his father a few days later.

"He was suspended with pay, which is our legal obligation to do," [School Communication Coordinator David] Mustonen said.

"As of (Thursday), [Mr. Ivan] has resigned from his position with Dearborn Public Schools."

During the sentencing of Ivan, and after a plea-bargaining agreement was reached, the mother of one victim pleaded with the judge for a maximum sentence. Ivan was sentenced to five years of probation, placed on the Michigan State Sexual Offenders website, and lost his teaching certificate. He was also terminated from Dearborn Public Schools. Other than Ivan collecting a salary while suspended, his termination did not cost the district a single penny.

Meanwhile, I had to resort to firing the last of the wrestling trio, Coach Narcis, after he deliberately disobeyed my directive and recklessly exposed student-athletes to a child predator, despite being privy to the allegations brought against Coach Bark. Yet with each effort I made to protect children, I only provoked more aggression from my enemy faction, including several who "served" on the Board of Education. In late July of 2007, for example—during my summer vacation—Trustee Shannon Drake contacted Dr. Artis to investigate my whereabouts. In her email to Dr. Artis, Trustee Drake deviously omitted the emails of Trustees Aimee Blackburn and Mary Lane, whom she knew had the best interest of all children at heart and who supported my efforts at Fordson High.

> From: [Drake, Shannon] <email redacted>
> Sent: Tue 7/31/07
> To: Artis, John B <email redacted>
> Cc: [All Trustees except Aimee Blackburn and Mary Lane]
> Subject: Fordson
> Hello again,
> Please tell me this is only a rumor. Is Imad in the Middle East again this summer? This has been told to me and I promised to check it out. Last year he was there to see a sick uncle; this year...if true, what is the reason, and has his salary been reduced accordingly? It is also my understanding (rumor) that his staff did not know until Monday. If the contract has been violated, then there

is a problem... there should NOT be special consideration given unless there is a letter of agreement and the Board is aware and agrees with the exception. I have not received a copy of the administrator's contract. The book I have is out of date and I would like one ASAP. I am willing to pick it up. I will get it tonight if left at my seat in the Board room. This would be the best way; however, if you are not able to do this then I will pick it up.

Thank you,

[Shannon Drake]

Astute to her tactics, Dr. Artis included in his response the absent Board members who should have been CC'd:

From: Artis, John B <email redacted>

Sent: Tue 7/31/07

To: [Drake, Shannon]; Board of Education Members

Subject: RE: Fordson

[Shannon], I am on vacation. However, generally, administrators work until the end of June. High school administrators do work a couple of weeks in July. All administrators return on August 20th. I do not know whether Imad is currently in Lebanon. I don't control administrators' time away from their jobs. When I return, I will get a copy of the contract for you.

John Artis

Later that night, Trustee Blackburn responded with the following:

From: Blackburn, Aimee <email redacted>

Sent: Wed 8/1/2007

To: Artis, John B; [Drake, Shannon]; Board of Education Members

Subject: RE: Fordson

John,

Is this an issue because of Lebanon, or are principals not allowed to go out of the state at all? Who is supposed to be notified when an employee goes on vacation? And does the notification require travel plans such as destination? If this is true, I would be interested to know where all of our staff went over the summer break. Could you get me a report on this?

Thank you,

Aimee

Then Trustee Lane chimed in (shortened for brevity).

From: Lane, Mary <email redacted>

Sent: Wed 8/1/2007

To: Artis, John B; [Drake, Shannon]; Board of Education Members

Subject: RE: Fordson

To all:

As we all know, the Board of ed is composed of seven fully elected members, each with equal standing and authority, acting legally only as a body, not individuals. All of the Board is entitled to be included in official district business and discussions... It is disrespectful, shows a lack of equal treatment to all trustees, and endangers the Board's ability to act as a whole, to deliberate without all's knowledge ...

E-mail conversations [from which] Aimee Blackburn and I [were] deliberately excluded violate these premises ... I am offended at being excluded from the e-mails entitled "Fordson" (but inquiring about Imad Fadlallah's whereabouts and time on contract). I have told Trustee [Drake] so, as well as President [White] ... I thank Dr. Artis for forwarding to Aimee and me.

While it is a legitimate question for a Board member whether a district employee is performing according to their contract, it is a factual issue and should be a straight-forward question. There should be no incursions into personal family life, which seem to me to border on possible illegal harassment ... E-mails are official district business; they are FOIA-able and available to the public. Thus, they should be fact-based and neutral in tenor. Sarcasm and maliciousness are inappropriate ... Further, each of us has a moral obligation to utilize public research resources when possible, which means availing ourselves of that which we can obtain [ourselves] without relying on others to do research for us.

Mary Lane

This prompted Trustee Drake to respond as follows (shortened for brevity):

From: [Drake, Shannon] <email redacted>
Sent: Wed 8/1/2007
To: Artis, John B; Board of Education Members
Subject: RE: Fordson

Dr. Artis,

As a Board member, I will not be asking you any more questions... I will let the rumors fly and the newspapers print rather than start WWIII when I ask a simple question. I will let them come to the meeting and ask while we are on TV... I thought it was pretty good that I asked you rather than let that happen. There is plenty of bad talk already about certain schools and situations, so I thought that since I was going to remain a part of the Dearborn community for the rest of my life that I would do what I could to stop any more negative stuff from being publicly asked. I will be here, and you will not, and I thought that it was very important that since the city was hiring a local marketing group to market Dearborn and the schools, I would try to stop it before it became a huge issue. Silly of me. I still don't have the answer... I thought that as a Board member, your boss, if you remember, I could ask a simple question and get an answer... don't worry... I will not waste your time in the future.

[Shannon]

Shortly thereafter, Drake fired off another email (shortened for brevity).

From: [Drake, Shannon] <email redacted>
Sent: Wed 8/1/2007
To: Artis, John B; Board of Education Members
Subject: RE: Fordson

In response to Blackburn's comments... I don't care
who goes where on their vacation. My question to YOU
was, "Is the vacation during the contractual downtime
for an individual?" I asked you so that I could stop a
rumor if indeed it is a rumor. ALL employees, regardless
of rank, in the district are expected to abide by their
contracts... It is funny that when I ask a question of
you it goes all over the community.

From: Artis, John B <email redacted>
Sent: Thu 8/2/2007
To: [Drake, Shannon]; Board of Education Members
Subject: RE: Fordson

Mrs. [Drake],

As superintendent, when a question is sent to me and to
only a portion of the Board of education, I believe it is my
responsibility to ensure all Board members are included.
I do not "send your comments all over the community"
as you imply, but I do believe all Board members should
be operating from the same information...

Regarding contract language and potential violations,
of course we check the contracts and time used. High
school principals are on a 46-week contract.

I currently have no knowledge of any principal who is
not fulfilling his or her 46-week contract.

John Artis

Nearly one year later, in May of 2008, a board hearing was organized to explore the ongoing allegations brought against me, including one that I slapped a student, the sound of which was allegedly heard 15–20 feet away by Mrs. Wix. Although I did not attend the meeting or request any support, over 500 people showed up to refute these baseless claims and endorse my efforts to reform Fordson High—a turnout that was organized by students, teachers, parents, and community allies. It became clear to Trustees Shannon Drake, Patty White, and Mariah Purge, as well as the army that they led, that the truth would need to be on their side if they wished to character-assassinate me.

Mr. Price, however, felt manipulation and bribery would work just fine. He pulled Jamal—a student who had an altercation with Coach Zaban—aside and asked him, "Did Mr. Fadlallah slap you?" Jamal initially declined this allegation, but after persistent manipulation by a team of staff members (and one student), he would fabricate a story that this was true. Later, in his written testimonies about each staff member involved, Jamal confessed that he was pressured by teachers to fabricate this story:

> "[Mr. Price] kept insisting, '*I* heard he slapped you! How long are we going to let this happen? He gets

away with this... how many kids can he slap before he gets in trouble?' I explained that I already consulted [other adults] and resolved the issue. [Mr. Price] smiled, laughed, and stated, 'They screwed you! It was a setup.' Then, he told me to go to the police station and file a police report; and [then] attend the Board meeting and tell them what happened. When walking in class, he patted [me on] my back and said, 'Don't worry grade-wise... we'll fix that for you.'"

Jamal also stated that Mr. Price repeatedly lectured students about how "This administration is screwing you guys over," adding, "He said it like seven times in just that one class period." Then there was Mrs. Stern, who summoned Jamal to her office:

"She looked at me with a sad face, as if she was shocked and horrified. She began to speak with a soft tone. This pisses me off. She covered her mouth (mouth wide open) with her hand and said, 'HOW could he do this!?' I just looked down as if I was hurt. She said, 'You know what I would make you do if you were my son? Go to the Board meeting tomorrow...' At the Board meeting, [Mrs. Stern] was determined. She grabbed a blue card and handed it to me. I hesitated and left, saying I was looking for a pen. She followed me and gave me a pen. She stood over my back and dictated [to me] what to write [and] say."

Then there was Ms. Sarah, who approached Jamal at the Board

meeting and "pointed out the Fadlallah supporters": "These guys are the ones you should talk to…they are on your side, and the others are against us," she said.

Then there was Mrs. Prime, who had never spoken to Jamal before this incident. Jamal's testimony reveals that—after summoning him to her classroom for a private discussion—she stated the following:

> "I heard Fadlallah slapped you. I filed a report to human services. I have a lawyer that is going to battle this out with Fadlallah. I have met with a [State] Representative on this issue and I want the right thing to come out of this. All I need from you is to write down that Mr. Imad Fadlallah slapped me [and] your name, ID number, and signature."

According to Jamal, he refused to sign, and Mrs. Prime became frustrated and determined to secure his signature. She assured him that she would press charges against me if I tried to compromise his stance.

And when it wasn't the teachers, it was a fellow student who worked with Mrs. Stern and who, according to Jamal, "had obviously been pulled into her beliefs." The student pressured Jamal into visiting the police station, to no avail.

In a May 2008 *Arab American News* article titled, "Community Backs Fordson Principal Fadlallah: Hundreds Attend School Board Meeting," Delia Habhab summed up the issue in this manner:

> "While many in attendance were relieved that Fad-

lallah was cleared of the assault charge, they were eager to confront the larger issue of the role that the small group of staff members played in the conspiracy against him. The same staff members have allegedly made disrespectful and discriminatory remarks to Arab and Muslim students about politics and/or religion on a regular basis, and parents say their continued harassment has led to a hostile environment that is detrimental to the students' learning process. The general sentiment among community members was that something needed to be done to put an end to the ongoing harassment and malignant treatment that the students were being forced to endure."

Instead, the harassment persisted, and the lawsuits poured in, even years later. This article was published in the *Dearborn Press & Guide* on August 5th, 2009. I've shortened the article for brevity and bolded key statements for emphasis.

Fired Fordson Coach Files Suit Against DPS, Principal

By Katie Hetrick

DEARBORN – [Nick Narcis] claims in a federal lawsuit that he was fired as Fordson High School wrestling coach for religious reasons. [Narcis] is suing Dearborn Public Schools and Principal Imad Fadlallah, claiming Fadlallah, a Muslim, forced [Narcis] out because of his affiliation with a volunteer assistant coach who was also a minister and [who] converted a student from Islam to Christianity.

The school district is not commenting on the suit [that] seeks to have [Narcis] reinstated, [with] back pay for the year of coaching he missed and attorney fees.

[Narcis's] termination after 35 years of coaching was entirely about religion, his attorneys say. "It's Principal Fadlallah interjecting his faith in an inappropriate way on Coach [Narcis]," said [Braxton Stillman] with the Thomas More Law Center. The Ann Arbor-based center "defends and promotes America's Christian heritage and moral values." The center provides its services for free. **The suit alleges, "[Narcis] was unceremoniously terminated from his position because he is a Christian..."**

According to the suit, Fadlallah became enraged when volunteer assistant coach [Bob Bark] converted and baptized a Muslim student during a summer training camp unconnected to the school's wrestling program.

The principal gave [Narcis] the "nonsensical edict" of keeping [Bark] out of the school and away from the wrestling team, the suit said.

Fordson is Dearborn's largest high school. Most of its students are of Middle Eastern descent, and many are Muslim. **The suit claims Fadlallah, since his appointment as principal in 2005, has systematically tried to weed out Christian school employees.**

School Communication Coordinator David Mustonen refused to speak specifically about [Narcis's] case, but [he] said principals have discretion about hiring coaches and similar positions within their building.

"It is the prerogative of the principal to make decisions on those positions," he said.

The suit argues that Fadlallah's Muslim faith was the driving force in his actions toward [Bark] and then [Narcis]. The documents also say Fadlallah was so upset about the student's conversion that he "punched the student in full view of students and faculty."

Dearborn Schools last year received, investigated, and then dismissed a complaint that Fadlallah slapped a student.

"It was found to be totally false," Mustonen said. Reports at the time said the district could not find any witnesses to the incident and the student eventually dropped the complaint.

As a coach, [Narcis] earned more than 450 wins, was elected to the Michigan High School Athletic Association Hall of Fame and was named "Sportsman of the Year" by the All-American Athletic Association.

[Marcus Chump], president and chief counsel of the Thomas More Law Center, said in a press release, **"We are getting a glimpse of what happens when Muslims who refuse to accept American values and principles gain political power in an American community. Failure to renew Coach [Narcis's] contract**

had nothing to do with wrestling and everything to do with religion."

Perhaps Narcis felt empowered to file suit after garnering such strong support from the DPS Board of Education in the months and years leading up to it. Here is a correspondence between Trustee Patty White and Nick Narcis. I bolded statements for emphasis.

From: [White, Patty] <email redacted>
Sent: Tue 5/13/08
To: [Narcis, Nick] <email redacted>
Subject: RE: Board of Education - Web Comments
Hi [Nick],
I am very sorry for this ordeal you are going through. There are very big problems at Fordson, and somehow this district has to stop protecting their "favorites" and deal with the truth. My hope is a new superintendent will do so.
Meanwhile, I will personally look further into this matter. **I have been asked by the ADSA to meet with Imad because he is so distraught over what he is enduring. I'm not sure I want to do that. Maybe bamboo shoots under my fingernails would be more pleasant!**
I really believe Imad has become a liability to the district. This must be resolved.
-[Patty]

From: [Narcis, Nick] <email redacted>
Sent: Tue 5/13/08

To: [White, Patty] <email redacted>
Subject: RE: Board of Education - Web Comments
Hi [Patty],
Thank you for your response. I will not sit quietly by
while Fordson is crumbling. The right people have to
be in the right positions.
Grateful,
[Nick]

Meanwhile, Trustee Mariah Purge continued to conspire
against me.[32]

From: [Purge, Mariah] <email redacted>
Sent: Tue 5/13/08
To: [Narcis, Nick] <email redacted>
Subject: RE: Board of Education - Web Comments
I am hearing you [Mr. Narcis]; the Fordson contingency
may have opened too wide a door this time. If those
voices on your side grow more public, as we have been
asking, I am there to help rectify the situation. Strength
in numbers works both ways- but be mindful that, of
late, the ACLU (I believe a local Muslim is on their Board)
has been a strong supporter of Arab issues, and church
v state has been twisted to work only in their favor.
Best wishes,
[Mariah Purge]

---

32   As of 2024, Purge continues to "serve" on the Board with a clear
bias and agenda against our Arab and/or Muslim community.

From: [Narcis, Nick] <email redacted>

Sent: Tue 5/13/08

To: [Purge, Mariah] <email redacted>

Subject: RE: Board of Education - Web Comments

Thank you so much for understanding the mess that is besieging Fordson. Also, I want to thank you for the heads up on the ACLU. I'll be more diligent in the future.

Grateful,

[Nick]

As this exchange reveals, rather than prioritizing the safety of our children and serving as an objective member of the Board—a board that should have acted as a trusted confidant and cautious jury amidst these crimes—Mrs. Purge instead used her elected position to collude and connive while fueling tension across religious lines.

Worse yet, this was despite Trustee Purge's first-hand experience with how I operated as a principal; for this was the same Purge who phoned me as a parent in panic, requesting my help one night during my tenure at Stout Middle School. Her daughter Annabelle, a then student at Stout, left home after school hours and was nowhere to be found well into the night. I threw on my jeans and sped from East Dearborn to the west side where Stout was located, and where I began visiting the homes of students to track Annabelle down. I interrogated one student, Anthony, in front of his parents—since I had a strong hunch he could help. Eventually, he cooperated; and within a half-hour, he helped me track down Annabelle, who was asleep in the basement of a boy's home until I woke her up and drove her to the Purge residence.

Yet Purge—who was as thankful as any parent would be that night, and who knew I treated Annabelle with the same care I extend my daughter and every other child in my school building—was now irresponsibly and dangerously meddling with my duties to protect children and assist with a criminal investigation. Blinded by bigotry, Purge sided with Mr. Narcis from the get-go, without due process.[33]

Nevertheless, I was tasked by Superintendent Dr. Artis (who had no other choice in the matter) to formally respond to a slew of allegations, both new and old. Another hour or two that should have been dedicated to our children was spent attempting to diffuse the fumes of hatred and lies. I've shortened the following email to Dr. Artis for brevity.

John,

Here we go again. Here goes another witch-hunt

---

33   Purge's attacks on Principal Fadlallah continued even after his death. During the DPS Board of Education meeting on February 11, 2019, Board President Purge interrupted then Trustee Fudwa Hammoud's glowing remarks about Principal Fadlallah—including Hammoud's recommendation that a school building be named after him—with the following words: "But you can't speak that way. Quite frankly, every person hasn't had those experiences; you're making a broad generalization that everybody in the community has shared those experiences." Tensions flared between President Purge and hundreds of attendees who were there in support of Mr. Fadlallah's legacy. Nevertheless, the board voted unanimously in favor of naming the Stout Team Room and Fordson Atrium after Imad Fadlallah, thus setting new precedent by memorializing an administrator across two school buildings.

propelled by alleged fears and phobias resting on mere insinuations and faulty interpretations. This is not the first time, as you well know. I have a feeling that this will not be the last, either. Here go more speculations to taint my decisions with allegations [based on] race, religion, or cultural background. Here we go again.

As I have been directed by you to respond to [Mr. Narcis's] email, I will be revealing some, not all, confidential information about students whom I have made every possible effort to protect in this process. My decisions continue to be based solely on *facts;* and here, sir, are the facts:

- In September of 2005, the athletic director, [Mr. Stern], brought to my attention that [Mr. Bark] filed a police report against a teacher at Fordson alleging sexual misconduct against a member of the wrestling team.

- I invited [Bark] to a meeting in the presence of [Stern]…[Bark] would not reveal [a thing].

- After an exhaustive investigation, I was able to determine the teacher involved and turn the matter to HR.

- Later in the school year, I received a three-page complaint from a 14-year-old student alleging that he was driven by [Bark], without parental consent, to Port Huron. [There, Bark] had his son push him underwater [and] his daughter take pictures of the incident. Then [Bark] threatened the student to expose him in the community and post his pictures on the web if he denies he is a baptized Christian.

- Based on these facts, and on his own admission, I terminated [Bark's] volunteer services as a wrestling and football coach at Fordson and clearly directed him, in a letter that I handed to him personally, not to be in contact with students at Fordson.

- Based on the complaints of several parents, [Bark] continued to be actively involved with the wrestling team.

- I proceeded to terminate the services of [Narcis] since he refused to cooperate with me to limit [Bark's] involvement with wrestlers.

- [Mr. Stern] appealed to me to grant him another chance after we met in my office and [Narcis] assured me that he will follow my directive.

- I continued to receive complaints about [Bark's] direct involvement with the wrestling team and about [Narcis's] derogatory remarks to students.

- In the meantime, the teacher who was accused of sexually abusing students had his day in court where he admitted to sexually abusing two students.

- Yes, I have been trying very hard to keep this quiet. I still feel the kids should be shielded from this controversy.

- I begged several PTSA parents who were in the process of distributing flyers in the community accusing [Mr. Bark] of being a religious predator not to do so for the sake of the students.

- I am "guilty" of conducting a thorough investigation on my own which led to the firing of [Bark's] buddy at a time when the Wayne County Prosecutor Mr. Dan Less and Lieutenant Hayse from Melvindale Police informed me that they are dropping the case.
- I am "guilty" of terminating the services of [Mr. Bark] who clearly admitted in his own words that his mission was to convert kids through wrestling.
- I am sorry there are many other issues I cannot and will not write [about].
- As far as the other accusations that "I slapped a student" and a teacher "heard the slap:" This teacher, [Mrs. Wix], is the same one who filed a petition accusing me of an anti-Christian agenda when I terminated the sexually abusive teacher [Ivan] from the building and when I terminated [Mr. Bark].

Please, Dr. Artis, advise your Board not to skate on thin ice. You will be conducting another investigation based on:

- Someone "hearing" a slap
- Stopping a [teacher] survey for "religious reasons"[34]

---

34 This survey, administered to students in class, was designed to match male and female students with one another based on dating preferences.

- [Teachers phoning] protective services on the principal for "abusing kids"
- "Not flying the US flag"[35]
- Flying to Lebanon again
- Driving "the good teachers" out of Fordson
- Refusing to allow the police into the building
- Coaching staff [allegedly] making obscene gestures at the other team
- Eliminating policies that keep students outside the classroom
- Giving the parents a voice...

Just imagine what any reasonable person, not necessarily an attorney, would say about conducting another investigation based on, "I heard a slap." Here, I would really like to ask why a slap loud enough to be heard 15–20 feet away wouldn't leave a trace or a mark on the student's face? I am truly tired of being investigated and I think it is time I do some investigating myself.

And so, despite many beautiful memories and triumphs throughout my tenure at Fordson High, the reality of my role was that I became consumed with court summons and sleepless nights spent composing emails like the one above. At times, it felt like I was losing the battle of beliefs in the bigger tug-of-war that would define whether students would

---

35   A lie fabricated about Principal Fadlallah after the flag pulley broke, causing the flag to lower.

be freed or remain incarcerated. My belief in our students gave me strength to pull on this rope with all the might in me, and to recruit as many allies as possible to join this cause. Yet staring across the other side of that rope to witness teachers and leaders—and in some instances, even student victims of manipulation—fight to keep their prison erect and occupied, was a disturbing reminder of the extent to which deviance, deceit, and hatred can stifle a community. Though I always believed—and still do—that the truth will prevail.

PART II

PRISON OF MY MIND

"The governance of wicked people humiliates noble people."

-Imam Ali ibn Abi Taleb (as)

7. HOMESICK

The wheels on the plane touching down in Minneapolis, Minnesota marked my arrival into adulthood, as well as my first chance, at eighteen, to escape the depressing, dungeon-of-dreams that Dearborn had become for me. My football field of failures as a Fordson Tractor would soon be replaced with a new field of dreams. But I had transformed my Tractor into a battle tank that I rode recklessly into my future, firing missiles of self-destruction at all the blessings trying to come my way. These missiles came in various forms of self-abuse, misguided choices, toxic media, and an allergy to academia. I was traveling on a shaky bridge over troubled waters toward a world of new opportunities, each coming at a hazardous cost as I tried to counterbalance my ignorance and homesickness with heavy hopes of a better future.

My ignorance was the israel to my Lebanese Shia identity—an identity I had lost like my roots in the occupied village of Ainata where Baba descended from. Lost: like the ~1,300 innocent lives brutally murdered in the July War just a month before I landed in Minneapolis in 2006, when I convinced Osama—my longtime friend and neighbor—to visit *Libnan*[36]

---

36 Lebanon.

with me for his first time. Lost: like me and "Oss," as we wandered the village of Brumanna where we escaped with my family to hide in a tall hotel whose large windows rattled from the Earth's quaking as each israeli missile landed miles away.

In Baba's room, me and Oss could sense the silent fury— the palpable pain of Baba's spectator guilt. He was heartbroken after leaving our village home in Qulaile where he sat stubbornly during the war until days before israel struck our land, leaving our windows shattered and a missile lying wait in our yard. And now he refused to leave Libnan, torn between unrealistic hopes of defending his homeland, and his reality, for he was "Commander in Chief" of his own sort of war 6,000 miles away in Dearborn where, on an immigrant's limb, he found himself fighting to live, then living to fight for the families of Fordson High.

But today, at least emotionally, Baba was a wounded warrior, and me and Oss sat alongside him watching live coverage of israeli soldiers bombing a school bus of children that burst into flames on the only road to Syria from where me, Oss, and my father's best friend Ibrahim (Mr. Elsaghir) would escape days later, followed by Mama and my sisters soon thereafter. As we prepared to pass the same location where those schoolchildren were slain, we read *Surah Al-Fatiha* before Oss extended me one of his earbuds, now split between my right ear and his left, as we let The Game's "Red Bandana" soundtrack that volatile road to Syria, polluting our prayer with poisonous lyrics that might've defined our last waking breaths. I'd later brag about the blessing I was powerless over.

Yeah, oh yeah khayeh, I'm dangerous
Arab intellect: redefining what danger is
War torn roots; come from where everyday is risk
Laser ish, 06' me n' Oss almost met the grave
Prayed to God to save it after all He gave us it
We were brave and ish
ʙᴜᴍᴘɪɴ' Game as we escaped
Grenades, planes, hysteria
In a van to Syria
                    -*Yallah, 2013*

It took us three or four days to arrive home to Dearborn. Within weeks, I said my goodbyes to Oss before boarding that Minneapolis flight, knowing I wouldn't see him again for months. But it was only a matter of days before I reunited with him in an unpredictable and most disturbing manner.

I had barely exited Minneapolis' airport before my brother Mac was teaching me to read maps, transfer between busses and trains, schedule classes, set up a bank account, wash clothes, use a credit card, eat a Chipotle burrito, and navigate a campus of over 50,000 students.

Daily, I would catch the 16 bus-route to school and back or ride the light rail transit into 5th Street where I was one among a sea of people who poured out into Downtown's vibrant grid. Glass tunnels intersected overhead in the sky like a scene in a futuristic sci-fi flick: corporate people in suits with briefcases commuting through glass skyways to their offices, restaurants, hair salons, and drycleaners—all on tile and carpet versus concrete.

New-student orientation was a spectacle, but it sucked the energy out of me like a flu, and when I walked into our apartment I had barely uttered "yo" before Mac pointed and yelled, "Ali, come here, *hurry!* Look who's on CNN."

And that was how I saw Oss again: orange prison suit. Head down. Eyes toward his headline of terrorist allegations. Hands cuffed to the front. The same hands that threw me touchdowns in my backyard as a seven-year-old; the hands I relished watching from my junior bench as they caught TDs and interceptions and carried many a basketball team into district championships as a poised point guard. Those hands were now shackled as he stood alongside our brother Ali "Ski" Houssaiky, Fordson's legendary all-state running back— known for somehow emerging out of a crowd of defensemen in a one-armed bear crawl with his Fordson yellow unstained as fans leaped from their benches in roaring excitement, now humiliated on national news in all-orange like our rivals at Dearborn High.

My heart sank as Mac flipped channels, allowing the story to unfold, each station propagating suspicion that Ali and Oss were buying TracFones[37] from Walmarts and RadioShacks to ship overseas for use in detonating bombs. Terrorist allegations

---

37   Pre-paid phones from the company TracFone Wireless, Inc.

on CNN. Traitor accusations on MSNBC. Felony charges of epic proportions.

Fear filled my heart. I didn't know about Ali and Oss's trip, but I knew the allegations were lies. I knew Ali and Oss were just two among dozens in Dearborn and across the Midwest who were buying TracFones for cheap out of state, and reselling them for profit to make ends meet. Though neither the truth nor the legal system ever proved to be on our side, so I wasn't sure I would see my brothers again. Meanwhile, Detroit's media had already mobbed our porch with mics and cameras in Baba's face:

"Are you Mr. Fadlallah, Principal of Fordson High?

"Any remarks on the terrorist allegations brought against Osama Abulhassan and Ali Houssaiky, alumni of your school? Do you believe they're guilty, sir?"

"Osama Abulhassan and Ali Houssaiky are kids that any parent would be honored to have!" Mr. Fadlallah shouted. "If they are terrorists, then my children are, too! Does *that* answer your question?!"

Baba was no lawyer or diplomat.

But escaping the White man's wrath with a name like Osama, as a "Hezbollah High" alumnus, just weeks after he spent his summer in his motherland where the *real* Hezbollah defended Libnan from israeli invaders, would require the families of Oss and Ali to afford attorneys skilled enough to ensure that "innocent 'til proven guilty" would apply even to those whom America was itching to punish.[38]

Meanwhile in Marietta, Ohio: America, powered by its media machine, was manifesting its highly anticipated day of judgment for the Muslim-Americans of whom the country was determined to rid itself. The USA had worked tirelessly in preparation for this day when it could make an example out of two ideal representatives: an "Ali" to serve as a reminder to his tens of thousands of namesakes—especially the Shia of Iran and beyond—of the prevailing superpower that is America; and an "Osama" to foreshadow the sweet taste of revenge against a Bin-Laden who it couldn't seem to track down.

Marietta's rural residents—many of them employed in either of the town's two chemical plants—practically bordered the bloodthirsty red state of Virginia, their location only symbolizing how "on-edge" they were. Ali saw it before he felt it: the Walmart clerk standing behind Ali's mother's car in the parking lot, jotting down the license plate while Ali checked out at RadioShack. The undercover cops hiding in plain sight at the bank as Ali and Oss filled their gas tank.

By the time they turned out of the station, Ali was all but certain danger was imminent, his intuition instantly confirmed when he and Oss were swarmed by four or five cop cars, followed by nearly twenty undercovers, as the harassment and

---

38   The passing of the 2001 Patriot Act granted unprecedented latitude to U.S. government officials to act upon mere suspicion of terrorism. No group was more impacted by this infringement on civil and human rights than Arab and/or Muslim Americans. This included spying, constant supervision of mosques and homes, arrest, interrogation, and even abuse, sanctioned by law.

hell week began—one that made Fordson football's "hell week" feel like a strawberry lemonade on spring break.

The German Shepherds were all but forced into uttering something after four rounds of orbiting Oss and Ali's car in silence—probably a bark of complaint provoked by tireless searching, or perhaps a choking yank on one of the leashes by the cop. Regardless, it was enough to justify the cops' unwarranted search. Twelve TracFones. $11,000 in cash. And the kicker: an airport manual from the Royal Jordanian Airlines Dept. at Metro-Detroit International Airport, where Ali's mom was employed part-time. Cops and detectives high-fived in celebration as they drove Ali and Oss to the station where the photographer barely let go of his shutter-button before their mugshots traveled like lightning to our Minnesota TV. They were shackled hand-to-waist, waist-to-feet, as they took baby steps toward their seemingly new destiny: a cage. But Fordson's prison of minds was no preparation for the real deal. Inmates smiled with a sense of familiarity as Ali and Oss walked past and stared back at them in utter shock. *How the hell do they know us?*

Recalling his experience on my sister Rima's *Dearborn Girl* podcast, Ali described when he and Oss were separated into glass pods, standing there like zoo animals for the rest of the inmates to salivate over, until Ali turned around toward the small television in the distance where it all finally made sense. He was now viewing himself through the eyes of me and Mac: orange prison suit. Head down. Eyes toward headlines of implied treason:

Is this an act of terrorism?

Large White men loomed, tattoos decorating their faces and bald heads, as they paced back and forth, their eyes fixated on Ali and Oss to intimidate them, while the Black brothers—who were more suspicious of law enforcement than of two Arab boys—offered a bit of comfort as they asked Ali and Oss questions in a more open manner.

The following morning, an officer approached Ali, requesting his paper containing the "obstructing justice" charge, crushing it up in Ali's face and throwing it out before handing him a new sheet, fresh off the printer:

"Soliciting for an act of terrorism"

And…

"Money laundering for an act of terrorism"

Seeing Ali for the first time in hours as he was escorted to video court, Oss seized the few seconds he had while passing his boy to coach him: "Plead the Fifth, Ski!"

It barely helped, as the same reporter from the day before rushed toward Ali after court:

"What do you have to say to the people?!"

To which Ali replied with his infamous line:

"I'm innocent. You guys are just being racist. I was just doing my job."

Hours later, from solitary confinement, Ali watched America's media machine work its black magic as it ran the clip of him saying, "I was just doing my job" on repeat—the first part of his statement omitted, and a new headline affixed:

What *was* that *job*?

That evening, Ali and Oss were placed in the same room. Inmates who passed by pointed fingers at them and laughed, picking up where the police had left off. On day four, Oss and Ali were finally allowed visitation with their families as they entered the visiting room completely shackled. The scene appeared as it does in movies, with two old phone booths divided by thick glass. Other than some familial tragedy, it was the first time both Ali and Osama saw their fathers cry. From his periphery, Ali saw the cop who had instigated the case watching from a distance with a ghostly facial expression, a mix of shock and confusion, perhaps wondering whether his apparent terrorist "home run" was in fact foul territory—completely out of bounds. The guard, however, was unflinching, laughing as he escorted Ali and Oss back to their cells and unshackled them. Ali stared the guard down like he would a linebacker: "I'm an all-state football player. I'm more American than you! How 'bout instead of laughin' you go and get us somethin' to eat or drink! It's been three damn days!"

The guard wiped the smile off his face and, to the surprise of Ali and Oss, returned with an ice-cold pitcher of water. It looked like a freshwater lake in a brittle desert.

But the relief was short-lived, as Ali and Oss awoke to news channels running old clips of explosions in Iraq, alongside pictures of their mugshots, leaving them weeping and terrified.

On-air with my sister Rima, Ali recalled, "At this point, I literally started to believe it; we are terrorists. The cops manipulated us to the point of believing we were guilty."

Baba would echo a similar sentiment in the multi-award-winning movie, *Fordson: Faith, Fasting, Football* released shortly after, and produced by media maven and ESPN affiliate Rashid Ghazi. Reflecting on 9/11, Baba said:

"In a way you feel you're responsible...or they make you feel that you're responsible, [as if] somewhere in the blood-trail you're related to those people that were on the airplane whether you like it or not. [But] this is not Islam, not Arabs, not any civilization with any sense of humanity in it."

Accepting the likelihood that Marietta would be his new home for a while, Ali took action: canceling the college courses that the TracFone profits should've helped pay for; phoning home to his older sister to insist she carry through with her wedding that coming week; and processing what his life might look like from here on as he battled Oss through countless games of paper football.

Meanwhile, Baba spent day and night at the home of Ali's parents, consoling them, warding off news anchors, leveraging contacts, and helping the family devise a plan. Detroit-based attorney Bill Swor connected the families of Ali and Oss with two more attorneys, based in Ohio. Collectively, the lawyers charged the boys a college-tuition-like sum to help prove their innocence. The Dearborn community raised nearly $300,000 in cash for the bond.

During days five and six, Ali and Oss continued to find refuge from reality in fantasy or paper football and discussions of the upcoming NFL season. Ali began reading—ironically enough—the biography of Sam Walton, founder of Walmart, probably during the same hours he should've been walking through its aisles to buy some new TracFones.

The hours felt like days until Oss was summoned to speak privately with his attorney, who said, "You guys will be out tomorrow. The prosecutors tried to pass the case onto the FBI, and the FBI basically told them, 'Hell no. You guys got yourselves into this mess, you can get yourselves out of it.' So, they have nothing. They're tossing the charges."

In an ESPN *E:60* special featuring Oss, Ali, and various participants involved in the case, an ESPN correspondent posed the following question:

"So, with all due respect, [Detective] Schneider—to your assistants—did the charge ever make any sense? The terrorist charges?"

"It didn't *to me.*"

"So how did your office become convinced that this was a legitimate charge?"

"I can't answer that question. I don't have a good answer for it."

To cover themselves, the prosecuting attorneys reintroduced the initial charge for obstruction of justice. And, for a short while, in those foreshadows of freedom, it seemed that justice was served for Ali and Oss. But emerging from those shadows into a new dawn would require them to do a lot more than simply leave prison.

"The after-effect was worse than being in there," Ali confessed on-air. "Endless media [outlets] around the world portrayed us as terrorists. Even people in the village back home began questioning my family."

Ali continued, "Growing up in Dearborn was a blessing and a curse. A blessing because culture was instilled—from people who look, act, [and] speak like us. We felt comfortable in 'the bubble.' But the curse was that we were blind to the perception people have of Arab-Americans. Outside of those [racist slurs] on the football field, I was ignorant. Even in Wyandotte [at the family gas station] I didn't feel it, but that's because I was in my comfort zone. I'm sure if I left the gas station and entered the neighborhoods, the target would appear on my back. My views changed after the incident because if I were White, none of this would've happened. I was ignorant to how my Arab identity painted me in a horrific light and led to me being targeted. I realized I would [continue to] be targeted. Psychologically, it had a huge effect on me. We go to Canada and they pull me over. They pull people over who have any affiliation with me and say, 'Who is Ali Houssaiky to you?'... even after I was found innocent. So, I entered a dark place in my life afterward. I realized my name was slandered. Even at twenty-seven it still bothered me... it kept creeping up, even when I was a teacher. One time I was [substitute] teaching at Livonia Churchill. I wrote Mr. Houssaiky on the whiteboard. A kid searched [my name] and [the incident] popped up. I got nervous and embarrassed. My heart isn't in education anymore because of that. I got a job offer, and they said, 'What happened to you in 2006?' Intuitively I felt something was off. That led me to pivot to business. Last summer I got pulled over with my two kids. Got interrogated. I said, 'Officer, I swear I was just singing different kid songs. I might've swerved.' He eventually let me go, but my heart was pounding. I'm still traumatized by it."

With the dust now settled in Marietta, Ohio, that Walmart employee never lived up her hopes of being a hometown hero. And in a way, Ali and Oss reemerged as our own Dearborn heroes as community residents rallied in the streets on the evening of their homecoming, awaiting their arrival alongside the same shameless news anchors who had just been antagonizing Oss and Ali's families.

And though it took years to recover, Ali would once again emerge from the cloud of his attackers and media slanderers in a one-armed bear crawl, opening one of Metro-Detroit's most celebrated eateries in King's Bakery, and finding himself on the news more often, this time to celebrate his family's award-winning recipes. He would marry his high-school sweetheart, find joy in fatherhood, deepen his faith, and begin expanding his King's locations—all while continuing to be featured on the likes of the Detroit Metro Times and the Netflix special, *Ugly Delicious.*

Likewise, Oss would rise above the drama as a dedicated father with a decorated career as an offensive coordinator and associate head coach for varsity football. He led Fordson football to its highest-powered offense ever, including its top-scoring season in Fordson's 90-year history. He inherited Coach Owl's varsity basketball program that held a 7–35 record over its two most recent seasons, and led the Tractors to four trophies in five years, including a three-peat of district championships. He was the center of the abovementioned ESPN *E:60* special, "What's in a Name?" and, more recently, the recipient of the 2022 Bill Walsh Coaching Fellowship, offering him a highly coveted coaching position in the NFL, where he joined the staff of Fordson alumnus and New York Jets head coach Robert Saleh. And so, the attempts to take Oss down with the New York planes proved petty—for despite years of turbulence, he rose above the ashes as a Jet.

But long before these triumphant days, I watched enviously from our TV in Minneapolis as my community took turns bear-hugging Oss and Ali in front of Detroit's media cameras, wishing I was there, too—my homesickness reaching record heights. I would have to wait months to return home myself as I let Baba's anger subside. For amidst false accusations brought against Ali and Oss, I was found guilty of a misdemeanor myself from a year prior when Oss bailed me out of jail, which had now resurfaced when our family was suddenly kicked off our auto insurance plan, prompting my father—who was just in his second full year as Fordson's principal, and who was beginning to learn that his and Mama's diligence could only shield us so much from Dearborn's drama—to investigate this so-called "crime" of which the insurance rep spoke. Baba was certain it was a mistake, until he called a Dearborn Police officer who showed up to Fordson hours later, laying on Mr.

Fadlallah's desk the mugshots of me and Izzy:

> See in town Baba's known all around
> So, I told lawyer, "Look, sir, this is how we gon' get
> down:
> Your only job is to make sure no-one knows
> Keep us fully covered
> And make sure that no-one blows!"
> Moved to Minneap, racked up a couple tickets
> Insurance lady calls Mama:
> "Your family's done, Missus"
> "Why?" she replied. "Tickets? A few times?"
> "Ma'am, your son's too much! Plus, he has a crime!
> Baba calls cops, he brings him my mug shots
> Thank God I was gone 'cause Ba blew his top
> And don't think I'm clownin' like I'm proud
> I lost my parents' trust—it wasn't in the lost n' found
> -Blueberry Mary, 2013

As I answered the phone from the East Bank of the U's campus, my stomach turned as Baba explored options: flying into Minneapolis to whoop my a**? Withdrawing me from the U? Shipping me to Lebanon? All the above! *"Lehh da'owsek!"*

My brother Mac unleashed his best lawyering to maintain custody of me, and for weeks, I kept my head down and my tail tucked, hoping tomorrow might be the day when the storm subsided and, most of all, praying my parents wouldn't learn the *full* story of what happened that day.

Tahoe in the impound, we in jail

Broke as *uh-oh,* five hundo for the bail
(Good look Oss); lookin' back what's most funny
More afraid of Baba than the fact I'm short money
To him weed is crack, no ifs buts ands
And if he finds out, my house might sound like band!
A.M.: Izz and me hit Mama's pharmacy in the D
He distracted her for me; I stole her ID
It's what I needed for the truck
                    -Blueberry Mary, 2013

I stepped out of Detroit's arrival doors and into the passenger seat of my father's car, greeting Baba cautiously, my anxiety loud on our quiet ride home. That would be the last time Baba picked me up for a while, as my boy Malik would be ready for me on future visits, including that one time we took a long detour into Detroit where we were stopped and the cop confiscated what was in the vehicle before sending us off. Or another on Greenfield Road on the Dearborn-Detroit border, when we had Ray—an older grad with a warrant out for his arrest—in the car with us. Once the police ID'd Ray, all three of us were thrown against the hood; but all they found was the stench of three typical Fordson boys, and only Ray was taken in.

Arriving home with Baba, I kissed Mama, whose baby face was colored with worry instead of makeup, and after wallowing in my parents' clouds of disappointment, I stepped outside and hopped into the backseat behind Kitch as Bous drove off. We did what lost kids in Dearborn do, switching between songs and storytelling, weaving through Dearborn and Detroit, from Outer Drive to Tireman, a typical night in the city. Until the conversation turned toward the Class of '05, then football, inching closer toward the unspoken stories of injustice we faced. And before I knew what was happening, the concrete walls of my emotions were penetrated as I exploded into tears—a horribly awkward thing to do in front of the boys.

My compensation for shrinking manhood was cuss words and full-force punches at the seat in front of me where Kitch sat as I questioned why he—one of the strongest players U of M's football camp had ever seen, Fordson record-setter for bench press reps of 225, heavy-hitting linebacker—wasn't given his rightfully earned shot, and why I wasn't either, and why so many others were robbed of theirs. Silence fell over them during my snotty soap opera, and for long after, only sparks of our cigs filled the gaps of silence for what felt like hours, until Bous took each of us home. But in our silence, I knew they felt my pain, not just 'cause I made my case, but 'cause they, too, carried some version of it with them all these years.

> Stopped by to say hi
> I know you lay low, 'cause you stay high
> You should quit too. *"For whaaattt?!"*
> I know your fear: the mirror ain't the same guy
> Who had it all at Fordson khayeh
> You had plans to make a fortune khayeh
> You ran 40s, track scorchin' khayeh

Then drank 40s fast as Porsche 11
Inshallah you recover, ride a Porsche in heaven
I just wonder if you see what I see
Dearborn drownin', see the tide? It's still a high-sea
January: say, "I quit!" Then: turn up for Pisces
Hope you catch my wave a bit?
When I see you, I don't wave; I sit
Care about you; love you; love your family
I lost it before; I fear for your sanity
Pill stash "just because" in your drawer?
Used to bet on dreams now you bet on the score?
Khayeh, what's this "too late" talk?
That's self-hate; you bit the devil's bait!
Let me settle…
Pistol in the air; let it smoke like a kettle
You were off to the races, medals on medals
You took 'em in stride, humble, gentle
Always smiles, laughs, now you're all shy
You say, "I grew up;" I say part of you died
You say, "I'm happy;" I say part of you cries
You might even believe it, khayeh; part of you lies
I see a suffering soul, no hope in your eyes
Hard guy disguise, broken behind
Hard guy khayeh, but you're broken inside
Deep down you're alive
Your spirit deprived
Intellect infinite but impoverished by highs
Your spirit deprived

Trade your highs for the highest khayeh; talk to your
Guide
Khayeh, I stumbled then fell
Fell again, then stumbled
Lessons on lessons, I was finally humbled
Ali vs. truth, I rumbled the jungle
Allah refereeing, all I had to was mumble (help)
Ring of the fast life, I learned nobody's fit
But this ain't your last life; don't *yolo*, repent!
God is forgiving
The Gift that keeps giving, khayeh
I see a better day... gotta fight, gotta pray
                    -Khayeh, 2014

"Ignorance is the worst kind of poverty, intellectuality is the greatest of riches, and reflection is the best form of worship."

-Prophet Muhammad (s)

8. STUPID

Except for those two recruits at Next Level Football Camp, nobody—especially a counselor—ever asked me where I'd go for college. Though college was a given for my parents, perhaps they also didn't ask because they hoped I'd find comfort in the local college scene like they had—especially after the drama of Mac's college woes. Maybe the rare sight of Mac's teardrops leaving grey dots on our white couch was still fresh in their mind. I remember that day when Mac visited from Albion. I was certain his homesick cry would coerce my parents to say, "Okay, habibi, stay home." But there was no huddle before Baba dropped the gavel: "You'll finish this semester at Albion. Then we'll talk transferring." Mac burst into tears as he heard the verdict.

So, if *Mac*—the academic prodigy—was begging to quit, I might not live to beg. But with senior year upon me, and my best friend Nass applying to U of M – Ann Arbor, I knew that for the first time in high school—at least for a prolonged period—I'd have to study. And now, more than ever, as my mind fogged in the face of numbers and my eyes recorded blanks each time they scanned a reading passage, I sensed that I was stupid. Very stupid.

With my high GPA exposed as the pretty mask of miseducation that it was, and the seed of my stupidity planted deep into my psyche, the evidence abounded. Like the day my ACT score of 21 arrived and Nass said, "Don't stress about it, bro. You couldn't apply to U of M anyway."

"What? Why not?" I asked.

"You don't have the two-year language requirement—no one told you, guy?"

Or the day I sat in my first classroom at The U and realized I couldn't do anything as well as the most lackadaisical White kid. Or the day of my first career fair, when I interviewed for a Target internship and the interviewer interrupted my long, awkward pause to dismiss me halfway through my twenty-minute slot with a dirty glance: "You're free to go." Or that March day, months later, when I finally heard back from someone after submitting fifty-plus internship applications, and I accepted my only offer in Brooklyn, New York, where I relocated for the summer to earn a $4 per hour stipend at the Brooklyn Children's Museum. I spent forty hours a week carrying ten-foot pythons and other reptiles on my neck and arms across Brooklyn to attract children to our museum tent, which I loaded and assembled myself—along with the snakes and other reptiles—at each new site.

Or that day during my senior year of college when I stared at my list of job application rejection emails, except one wait-list for Teach for America. Or the day I took an ACT practice test with my eleventh graders in one of America's lowest-performing schools in Clarksdale, Mississippi, and two students outperformed me—a secret I kept buried deep in my gut. Or the day I hired Chin, my GMAT tutor who prepped me for my MBA application and who—after a horrifying practice score and several stumbles over simple math—told me: "Ali, I'm not sure I can help you, my friend. I highly recommend the GRE; the math is much easier."

Or the day I stared back cluelessly at my MBA professor before he chastised me in an auditorium full of students since I didn't have an answer for his supposedly-basic question about supply, demand and China: "Well, I'm glad you're here getting an education, kid."

Or the day I failed my MBA accounting course. Or the day I interviewed for Harvard and was asked when my "formal education" began, and I stuttered nervously because I had no idea if that meant something other than *school?*

I left that interview certain I would be rejected, and after I flew back to Atlanta, I felt so miserable about my performance I skipped my MBA classes to fly home, hoping my parents could offer some words of consolation and perhaps inspire the "Plan B" I didn't have.

So, every accomplishment on my path, especially the academic ones, felt like an unlikely feat. Like in 2009 when I auditioned and was selected to be the commencement speaker for the University of Minnesota and stand before 4,000-plus students to represent a quality liberal arts education.

I found my serendipitous seat on stage next to our Vice Provost. "Wait... I *know* you," she said, just two minutes before I'd deliver my speech. I stared at her, trying to recall the familiar face, until she began pointing at me and smiling, moving her index finger up and down as her memory played back the snow-storming scene one night near midnight, miles from Minneapolis: "You're the young man who dug our tires out of the snow on I-35 a couple months ago! You and that young lady—wasn't that you?"

"Yes, ma'am, that was me."

It dawned on me that the likelihood of the person whom we helped rescue from the highway's shoulder being my Vice Provost—and thus being on that stage—resembled the likelihood of *me* being on that stage, seated next to her. And although, like the tires in that snow, I dug long and deep, past doubt and failure, and through the brutal cold to get unstuck and accelerate toward that stage, I knew exactly what—and who—was responsible for my unlikely triumph. It was the handful from the hundred-plus teachers and professors whose classroom seats I sat in who helped save me. The handful from Henry Ford Elementary, and the few from Woodworth Elementary and Stout Middle and Fordson High and college who fought—sometimes by fighting me—to awaken me from my deep slumber.

It was my militant mother, whose love was tough and stubborn; the visionary kind—when a mother chooses the future of her child over his friendship. She ignored my puppy-faced protests and set a minimum quota of summer books I had to read before I could hop on my bike. She sat me at the kitchen table to tutor me through science after standing on her calloused feet in Detroit's projects from 8 to 5. And not long after I entered the prison of minds, she printed vo-cabulary words and plastered them all over our house walls without announcement—kitchen, family room, stairways. The bigger shock was how little it phased her that our home's aesthetic went awry, so little that she didn't even place the packing tape on the back of the papers, just slapped it over the top diagonally, quite the lure for my lethargic mind, now resistant to reading and largely ignoring the words beyond a glance, though on occasion a word would pique my interest, like "PUGNACIOUS" in big bold letters, finding its place in our living room near the kitchen corridor: "eager or quick to argue, quarrel, or fight."

It was Mac, with his sharp insults that brought a pit bull's pugnacity out of me but who revised every college paper I sent him, providing me with detailed feedback and grammar lessons and teaching me how to build my résumé—not just on paper, but through experiences that would soon decorate it.

It was Abe Mashhour, my eighth-grade science teacher, who not only accepted my stanzas of rhymes as a form of extra credit, but wrote some back to me, nurturing my creativity by way of a collab.

It was Amira Kassem, who set up my desk in the hallway to discipline me as I stared at the ceiling for the first week of freshman English and who, for two more years, planted the seeds in me: "You write like you're thirty, Ali;" or "Love isn't two people just staring into one another's eyes, Ali, it's two people staring out in the same direction;" or, by way of a post-er in her classroom, "Practice doesn't make perfect; it makes permanent;" or most importantly, by way of a heartfelt email she sent me not long after I left Fordson High and entered the prison of *my* mind, "Contrary to what some believe, the Quran is a perfect book of truth, Ali. Never lose sight of that."

It was my tutor Chin, whom I turned to firmly and said, "Chin, just start by teaching me algebra and geometry from scratch" before he taught me the tricks of Indian math and we watched my GMAT score grow nearly 200 points before our bewildered eyes.

And of course, it was Baba, my principled principal, who groaned at my seventh-grade report card before handing it back to me, dissatisfied. Angrily, I protested:

"Ba, are you serious?! How can you be mad about a *4.0?!*"

He replied with one of those Imad-isms that would take me years to appreciate fully:

"Why? Because you're just getting by with your intelligence."

"So! Isn't that what I'm supposed to get by with?!"

To which I earned his best reply, that silent stare into my soul as if to say, *Search.*

His silent statements and words of wisdom, which carried me to Harvard, were like those he offered the night before my eight-hour interview, as I paced back and forth in my hotel room.

"Are you nervous?" he asked on the other side of the line.

"I thought I wouldn't be. But yeah. Very."

"Well, don't be."

He paused, gathering his thoughts—perhaps sensing that

my nervousness was actually terror—or perhaps just preparing to translate as he recounted a *hadith*[39] from Imam Ali (as).

"My advice for you is the same as Amir Al-Mumineen's advice to his soldiers before they entered battle: '*Mountains may move from their position, but you should not move from yours. Grit your teeth. Lend to Allah your head. Plant your feet firmly on the ground as though nails have been driven into them. Enter with a firm determination that you have lent yourself to the cause of God. With all this, remember, success lies in the hands of God.*'"

The *hadith* pierced me. The feeling of strength and spiritual fortitude it gave me was strange, since admittedly, I wasn't sure how relevant war instructions were to the eight-hour intellectual reckoning I was up against the following morning.

Until lunchtime the next day, when I felt like I was in round six of a boxing match with the intellectual equivalents of twenty-four Mike Tysons, and I *definitely* wasn't feeling like Muhammad Ali. Not even like Tarick Salmaci or Prince Naseem. I felt like gravity; I wanted to tap out. Or really, just run home and cry. And that was exactly when Baba's words— or more precisely, his reminder from Imam Ali (as)—tapped me on my shoulder: *Mountains may move. But I shouldn't. Grit my teeth. Lend my head to Allah. Success lies in His hands, remember?*

Let's go. Search, Ali, search. Finish strong.

I did. And my resolve helped me secure a full ride to one

---

39 Sayings or traditions (namely, from Prophet Muhammad, s.a.w.s., and his Holy Progeny, a.s.).

of the most competitive programs in the world.[40]

But despite Baba's prompts to "search," and despite the insistence that I was smart and capable, these folks—the Amira Kassems, the Chins, even Baba and Mama—were only a proof-point to me of how deficient I truly was. Because their actions spoke louder, for I watched them labor like an Olympic team who rallied around the rope of my destiny and pull until exhaustion so that I might emerge from the hole I was in.

And I would learn that no milestone or moment—not bringing Baba to tears by surprising my parents as the commencement speaker at the University of Minnesota; nor earning admittance into Teach for America's highly competitive program; nor being nominated for the National Sue Lehmann Award for outstanding teaching (an award my sister Rima, against more odds than me, would win years later); nor earning a top 20 MBA; not even a full-ride fellowship to Harvard University for my doctorate—could cure the feelings of insecurity, invisibility, inadequacy, and imposterism that were painfully etched, like invisible ink, into my self-image.

---

40   Two weeks after my interview, I flew home from Atlanta to Detroit. Just as I was preparing to enter a barbershop in Dearborn—and weeks before Harvard's decision date—I received the call. Being home for the news was almost as good as the news itself. It was the longest haircut of my life—I couldn't wait to drive to Mama's pharmacy to break the news, then do the same with Baba at home. When I showed him my phone, revealing a call from a "617" area-code, he looked at me with utter shock—waiting for me to confirm with a head-nod—before he ran away from me, bursting into tears, and praising Allah (swt).

"He who is ignorant deludes himself, and consequently, his present is worse than his past."

-Imam Ali ibn Abi Taleb (as)

9. SELF-HATING (ARAB)

For me to be among the first of our American kind—a Muslim, Shia, Arab, first-generation American-born Lebanese, hip-hop fashioned Fordson boy, who used words like "key" and "let me" in ways only few could decode—was a bizarre starting point for my identity. For one, I never saw a semblance of myself, or Dearborn, in mainstream media—the place where we were socialized to "find ourselves" in. We were nowhere to be found, not in popular music or politics, film, or fashion. Just think: DJ Khaled, 1,400 miles away in Miami, was the only almost-representation I felt I had. But it wasn't just not being seen for who I was; it was being seen *and hated* for who I wasn't—you know, America-hating terrorist, women-hating misogynist, Jesus-hating extremist, gas-station-bound barbarian, et cetera. It was a strange reality; one that became ripe soil from which my seeds of self-hatred took root.

It happened slowly, subconsciously, and surely—feelings of invisibility teetering on insanity. This insanity made me question whether I deserved to be seen—just like I once questioned whether I deserved to see the court or the field—and whether I should betray Baba and Mama's teachings and join the majority who already jumped ship on our sinking identity.

Many jumped into the "white sea"—the Mohammeds and Alis and Husseins of the west side, now Mike, Eli, and Sam. Though the east side was more inclined toward "blackness," doubling down on our Detroit-influenced identity in our own Arabized ways: Air Jordan slides with socks on to school, fresh fades, fitted caps, and names like "Killa Bous," "L.G.Unit" (Alaguli) and "Young Merce."

Whatever it was, I needed some workaround in a nation determined to erase my identity, to prostitute my faith, to persecute and remove the hijabs from my matriarchs, for America insisted that the liberation of Muslim women was tied up beneath that suffocating fabric. Its so-called progressive language was passionately crafted to belittle my ancestors and belie the true intent of America, for I would later learn that it just wanted to use my wife's hijab as a fashionable noose to hang us from.

My uncle Jihad, for one, is a little hard to erase at six foot four inches, 230 pounds, and one of the few childhood heroes I had—tall and short-tempered but a gentler giant who wore his heart on his sleeve and a clean shave, and who, along with my uncle Hassane, took me to Pistons, Lions, and Wings games, and performed miracles: catching bees and showing me their stingers without getting stung, introducing me to Isiah Thomas at courtside, then snapping the Polaroid selfie for proof. Jihad even convinced my parents to let me cruise with him to the Caribbean on a Carnival ship, where he kept calling me "chicken sh**" 'cause I was too shy to approach a pretty girl I kept seeing aboard. They were my biggest fans.

Jihad was even my photographer, the man who snapped shots of me snatching first-downs near the sideline, and shots of my jump-shot at the moment's flick of my wrist, following his calm still-shot with a roaring "Let's gooo!" that startled spectators and shook the bleachers.

The sound and sight of "Jihad" was one of jubilance, but America never knew my uncle, nor wanted to, for that matter. Though it claimed to. It re-introduced us to Jihad as the war-mongering barbarian whose "holy war" was to be waged against the West. America managed to dismiss Jihad as a legit name that mothers like my *teta*[41] give their child for reasons that have probably never once in history had anything to do with losing them on a suicide mission. Its media fought to sabotage the words of our Holy Prophet (s): "The greatest *jihad* is to battle your soul, to fight the evil within yourself."

And yet, in the same breath that it used to dismiss the name, America named 1.5 billion Muslims "Jihad" all at once, thrusting the term "Islamic Jihadists" into our global consciousness overnight. Its propaganda was like American police on a drug raid, and we were just lying in the dark on Dearborn's east side. We know how that story unfolds.

The silent slaughtering of our kind that happened in Dearborn for decades pre-9/11, became an international campaign post-9/11: a "war on terror" laced with Islamophobic rhetoric and characterized by the war on Iraq, domestic hate crimes (including many in Dearborn), new discriminatory laws and policies, airport harassment (of which Jihad and Hassane en-

---

41   Grandma.

dured the worst), and local abuse—no better an example than that of the City of Dearborn and its public schools, especially Fordson, where my sister Rima spent each morning watching fifteen minutes of Fox News, her teacher's replacement for the recommended fifteen minutes of silent reading. The teacher followed Fox with his monologues, criticizing "this administration"—code, of course, for Imad Fadlallah—for its horrible leadership, making a hobby of humiliating my then thirteen-year-old sister whose fear, mainly of adding to Baba's mounting stress, stopped her from reporting the monstrosities she endured.

And when it wasn't *that* teacher, she was fielding interviews from others: "Why does your father visit Lebanon so often? What does he do there? Why doesn't he come to your track meets? What's he like when he gets angry? Do y'all talk?"

So, I was alive—but not awake—for America's onslaught. I was among those who Imam Ali (as) described when he said, "People are asleep; and when they die, they awaken." I was, despite Baba's eloquent recounts of *hadith*, an empty shell of the spiritual knowledge our forefathers were armed with. I found no refuge or respite in knowing I was unfairly targeted, for "There is no poverty more severe than ignorance," Imam Ali (as) said, and the real refuge was in the proverbial caves of my history. "Knowledge gives life to the soul," he added.

But I wouldn't find these words, nor find myself in them, for another decade, and the light of my soul dimmed to a darkness that left me searching for lost truths amidst America's propaganda, its media slowly transforming my insecure reality into an identity crisis, one that beckoned me to share the bigot's sentiment, not so boldly as beginning to view myself or my kind as barbaric, no, but more discreetly and dangerously, as I privately wondered if maybe I belonged to a bloodline unfit for the Western lifestyle that my life was now styled in.

The evidence of my self-hate, as it goes, hid in plain sight. I dressed my words and myself to impress, but I dressed the wounds inside of me with binges of fast food and worse forms of abuse. "Fat" and "slow" were among the secret mantras my mirror evoked, even as I still believed I loved myself. And being powerful and known—being significant—were themes that captivated my conscience and career plans. My self-hate was a sure-fire, predictable—at least by default, if not by design—for Dearborn taught me that White folk were kings and queens of control, and hip-hop taught me that Black folk were kings and queens of culture, and so I should vie for validation from one or the other or both. And, more notably, it taught me that chief among my challenges was not existing at the bottom of this totem pole, but worse, not existing at all.

Yet, I couldn't locate my self-hate, 'cause I saw myself through the mirror America had fashioned for me, a distorted one of invisible cracks that was clever not to reflect them back; cracks of anti-Islam and anti-Shia and anti-Arabism and anti-immigrant that contorted my self-image like a carnival mirror. There were no application boxes to remind me to "check" on myself;[42] no literature to legitimize our struggle; no school statistics on Arabs to illuminate the gaps; no truthful media to mirror us; no figure to tell me, "Go figure!" or help me figure me out. All I saw was an Arab boy doing the best he could to play the game, build a career, build clout and eventually maybe earn a color in America's racial crayon box, 'cause *Brown* was already taken; and *White* was trying to white-out my culture like it did to Caucasians; and "olive-skinned" was a cute tagline, but whose race is that—the Grinch?

So even when I was intoxicated with internalized oppression[43]—a term that forever changed the way I viewed myself years later—and even as loved ones investigated why I was behaving as if I was immortal, I often saw a self-loving young

---

42   This refers to the absence of a race/ethnicity box on the US Census, on applications, or in reported statistics for people from Southwest Asian or North African (SWANA) descent, including Arabs. This impacts various aspects of our social, academic, and professional lives. To cite one example, policies and funding decisions at the governmental level, across sectors (including education), are often dictated by census data. No data means no representation; and no representation translates into minimal evidence to support the need for funding or policies that would target inequities faced by people of SWANA descent.

43   Internalized oppression is a term that stems from social justice theory and refers to the process by which members of an oppressed group begin to adopt (or internalize) the same views or actions towards their own group as those of the oppressor, thus acting against the best interest of themselves or their group. Changing one's ethnic name, removing beards or hijabs willfully and out of fear of being typecast as "too Muslim" (or from a desire to distance oneself from Islam), and associating lighter skin or eye color with beauty, are a few of countless examples.

man. For I was always smiling, equipped with Baba's content-edness and Mama's self-determination, bracing for blow after blow, accepting it as part of life, and refusing to abandon the seemingly unbroken boy who stared back. Instead, I turned my internalized scars into an invisible superpower that I used masterfully on my misguided path, scraping up clout or so-cial capital, using whatever privilege I could recycle from the White man's wasteland, albeit subconsciously: his pale white skin, check; his media to teach me how to climb his corrupt ladder, check; and of course, his money, the money that my poverty-stricken parents eventually earned and poured into my accounts so that I may hike to the highest of his higher-ed institutions. Checks.

But such hikes often come to a quick halt after high school, at least for most Fordson kids, and so I was privileged. While my boys back home got dressed for work, I might as well have put on a unicorn's uniform, 'cause I had the rare chance to escape the dogmas of Dearborn and roam free in Minnesota. I was now walking on an open canvas, painting my persona anew on a new campus—from small town *sahras*[44] to the big city stage, still lost but willing to stand out or conform like a chameleon, code-switching with Dearborn charm, immersing into many-a-culture at once, still loyal to baggy fashion and fitted caps and white fur coats with Timbos and old-school foam headphones playing a fire playlist, featuring the latest LimeWire downloads of Lil Wayne. I was emboldened by the reality that you couldn't "box me" like Muhammad Ali, 'cause

---

44   Late night get-togethers.

I was too invisible in society to have a comparable, and as I used my intuition to predict what box the next clown might try to place me in, I moved accordingly, dodging attempts to pin me down as I danced around many rings of social circles. Floating like a butterfly.

And yet, I laughed at the irony. I was far easier to pin down than any Minnesotan would ever know, because I had an unmistakable Fordson boy swag: stroll of an athlete, temperament of a loving Baba and a wise OG, tender but don't test me, a Dearborn kid functioning beautifully in his brokenness, like boxers or comedians whose art replaced the heartbeat of their struggle. My new ego was born, inflated with insecurity but feeling sizable nevertheless, and I was going to fly the high of that balloon until gravity brought me down.

I had enough time for five-ish of my favorite Wayne songs on my roughly fifteen-to-twenty minute walk across the breathtaking Washington Avenue Bridge that brought me from the U's West Bank over to the East. The bridge sat high above the immaculate Mississippi River that cuts the campus in half, capturing a gorgeous collage of awakened water, breathing trees, amusing architecture, and a stampede of students basking in the spacious glory of the U's campus.

It was on West Bank—the law school's home—where Mac found a flyer advertising an "alternative spring break" trip called the *Pay it Forward Tour*. He pulled it off the tack board for me and brought it to the apartment, where I stared at the campus group's name, *Students Today Leaders Forever (STLF),* and thought, *long name... but I like it*—not knowing STLF would soon play a central role in my college journey, and I would play my own tiny role in helping it grow into the nationwide nonprofit it became.

Within days, I was signed up and eating criticism between burrito bites at Chipotle from an animated "ATM," my Lebanese-Ghanaian brother Ahmed (now brother-in-law, too), whom I met in my first week at the U when I overheard him and his father speaking Lebanese slang at the corner store on campus, before introducing myself excitedly. That day led to a lifelong friendship, filled with fun memories of ATM being "Always Too Much"—proving his nickname was on the money. But on *this* day, ATM wasn't just over the top—he was under my skin.

"Ahh-lee, man, let me get this straight," He began. "*You're paying money...* to grab a shovel... and work for *someone else!?* During *spring break!?* He laughed until my death stare calmed him down. Then he continued pleading, "Fam-o, are you sure Mac told you to do this? Bro, it's *spring break!* Do they refund cancellations?"

I was first on the bus come departure day, wearing all black: my favorite sweatpants, long sleeve G-Unit thermal, a hair wrap over my curly afro, and an Oakland A's cap. I greeted the White folk who were prepping us for departure and strolled to the last row where I sat window.

162

I could sense the bus leader's nerves as she broke the ice: "You must be Ali? How are you?"

"Good, you?"

"Great! I'm Rachel Wax. Made-ja this cheesy name poster. Hope you like it."

She carefully taped it to the window, much unlike Mama's vocab words, as I replied, "I do, it's cool, thank you," wondering how she risked assuming I was Ali Fadlallah, until I realized I was one of two non-White kids—the other being an Asian girl—on the forty-five-person bus.

Hours in, I sat there mad as hell at Mac and salty that ATM was right. But within 48 hours I was high off intoxicants I'd never imagine, intoxicants I would lose all my street cred for if the boys were watching: camp songs; relationship-building circles; playing checkers with the elderly; serving hot plates to the homeless with a net on my head; painting walls; sleeping on YMCA and church floors in a sleeping bag; and most shocking of all, letting my walls down with White people who made me feel seen and loved. It was the rare breed of White which I had seen glimpses of in my childhood—the occasional Christine Schulkeys and Chuck Silvers of the city who you knew cared about you.

Within months, I was an STLF camp counselor and planning the first Pay it Forward Tour(s) for Dearborn and Detroit Public Schools, with help from Baba and my new Detroit friend Karinda, and from STLF's four founders, especially Irene—the Filipino prodigy from L.A.—and Greg, the captivating orator from North Dakota who led one of our buses full of Fordson kids, and who, afterward, despite having led many-a-bus of inner city youth, said, "Ali, I'm not sure how sustainable this is, my friend. This is the most challenging program experience I've ever had in my life."

"Man, I'm sorry, Greg. Fordson kids are...*different.*"

I walked away feeling embarrassed, even ashamed for not having better words to explain to Greg what I struggled still to understand myself. Was I surprised, even after knowing that a Cedar Point trip that my sister Rima had just co-organized resulted in the bus company suing Fordson High? Perhaps a wiser version of me would have tried to explain to Greg that the Pay it Forward Tour was—for us—like a bus ride into freedom after being trapped in the prison cells of Fordson's classrooms. Or that Fordson's culture was created by kids who felt so insignificant, they would do anything for fifteen seconds of fame; like Muhsin, a newcomer from Libnan, who always felt picked on by one teacher at Fordson, and who one day, was scolded and sent out into the hallway. The timing seemed too serendipitous since he needed to take a dump at that precise moment, and figured he should pay back the teacher by taking that dump right outside of her classroom door (of course, this "boater" became a legend).[45]

---

45   We often use the derogatory term "boater" to refer to newcomers. The term finds its roots in the journey of those like my *teta* Lila who arrived on American shores by "boat" (i.e., ship)—though it is equally applied to those who arrive by plane. For immigrant students in Dearborn Public Schools, the term "boater" signifies a double-plague: on one hand, poor education with limited English language support, and on the other, ostracization from bigoted teachers and bullying peers.

So, even though the students on the bus knew better, and although Greg was charismatic and genuine, he resembled their wardens. His white skin, blue eyes, and reddish-blonde hair were only a reflection of the power, leadership, and control that the Fordson kids were desperate to have over their own lives. Maybe, if I wasn't still internalizing so much of that myself, I could've articulated some version of that to Greg.

Nevertheless, I passed on the torch of Dearborn's Pay it Forward Tour(s) which continued for some time. Meanwhile, I joined and led countless college tours while helping to create a pipeline for more students of color to "pay it forward" over spring break—including ATM, who joined one of my busses before leading his own. Within a few years, I had visited fifty small towns I had never heard of and partnered with three others to organize STLF's first *Mystery Tour*, each destination of which was a surprise stop en route to New York City, where me, ATM, and the rest of us began our day as guests on *Good Morning America*. Right after, we hopped on our bus and drove to a maximum-security prison on Long Island, where we hosted a talent show that featured back-and-forth performances between us and the inmates.

Greg and Irene kept sending opportunities my way: new STLF experiences, connections for internships, and an all-expense-paid trip to San Francisco to attend *The Fundraising School*. I began writing and performing comedic raps to fundraise at STLF camps. A decade later, after Greg watched me recite a poem at Irene's outdoor wedding in Minneapolis, he invited me to deliver a TEDx Talk and performance in Fargo,

North Dakota, where he had returned to invest in his local community and where he founded TEDxFargo, one of the largest TEDx conferences worldwide. I would use my talk on "Hit Song Science" to discuss my complicated relationship with Lil Wayne, hip hop, and the music industry at large. Despite garnering over fifty thousand views and dozens of positive comments, the talk haunted me, for I would look back on it to see a young man who was still infected with internalized oppression: sporting pink jeans for a flare of fashion; using my best White voice with hopes of appeasing the North Dakotan crowd; and still seeking to find my identity in the very industries that helped me lose it.

One Monday during my sophomore year of college, I was standing outside Coffman Student Union when I saw a group of young Black men gathered in a circle, two of them with their arms around one another like homeboys, as they pointed at a brother before exploding into laughter that sent some of them running up the stairs, others squatting as they gasped for breath. A typical roast session, though one emanating a brotherhood that pulled me into a Dearborn daydream, more than any Minnesotan moment I had yet to have; 'cause even in the company of ATM, Sherief, Tony, and my other new Arab friends who became family to me, I was still a culture-departure from Dearborn, and I was missin' the boys.

"Who are they?" I asked, directing Murid's attention to the group.

"Those guys? Ha. Those are the Alphas!" He replied.

"What's that?"

Chuckling, Murid explained, "Alphas? Alpha Phi Alpha. The fraternity." He paused, sensing my interest, then said, "You gotta be Black to join them, dude."

"Really? Like, that's a rule?"

"I mean, if not officially, an unwritten rule." He said.

"Who told you that?"

"Dude, look at 'em!" he said, laughing. "Plus, I thought you were against the whole fraternity thing?"

Well, I was mostly talking about those beer-pong-playing, run-around-campus-naked frats, bro, I thought. But I simply nodded.

As the weeks passed and I kept hearing of respected leaders on campus, a pattern emerged: many were Alphas. So, when I saw Brother Kado setting up a table at the student org fair on Washington Avenue Bridge, I stopped by to chat; and when I ran into one of the "bruhs" at a party days later, I approached:

"Hey bro, you're John Hardy, right?"

"That's me," John affirmed. "What up, dude?"

"I want to be an Alpha." I said, firmly.

"Say what?"

"Yeah."

"You know what that means?" he asked, shocked at first, then smiling.

"Yeah. I think so."

"You own a suit?"

"Uh, yeah? I got one, I think, yeah."

"Aight, cool, cool. Take my number and keep in touch."

It was at least a year before I was blindfolded and led into a dark room where I stood in my all-black suit as a brother uncovered my eyes, only for me to be instantly blinded again, this time by the high-beam spotlight pointed toward my face so that the fifteen-plus brothers who sat around a long conference table could see me without being seen as they began firing questions at me.

One brother opposed the idea of a non-Black initiate, especially given that the only other one was brother Khalil who was dark-complected. He didn't hide his concerns.

"So Ali, what makes you different than Phinny?" he asked, drawing laughs from the bruhs. He was referring to the White brother who pledged Kappa Alpha Psi, another historically Black fraternity on campus, and I didn't care for the comparison.

"I'm afraid I don't understand your question, sir," I said, drawing *ooos* from the bruhs who knew that wasn't true.

"Did you not hear me, or do you not understand?"

"I heard you. I just don't think I have any more in common with Phinny than you do, sir, so I don't understand the question."

Bruhs erupted into a mix of laughs, *ooos*, and side-chatter, until one of the more senior brothers calmed down the group to ask more openly, "Can you speak more to why you feel Phinny is an unfair comparison, Ali?"

"Because when Phinny walks into a store, he's there to buy, and when y'all walk into a store, you're there to steal, and when I walk in, I'm there to blow that sh** up. *Sir*."

The bruhs fell silent. Some, perhaps, were shocked by my audacity. Regardless, I suspect most of them resonated with my words. After all, the bruhs knew how badly I wanted to be an Alpha, and my attitude in The Spotlight Interview was putting me at risk of early expulsion at worst, or a grueling initiation at best. But I wanted to be clear that although I saw myself in Alpha, I wouldn't let any Alpha un-see me in return. I was triggered and the Fordson boy was out.

In retrospect, I realized I was angrier about the idea of being gaslit by another brother of color than I was about being demoted by White men my entire youth. I was still prepared to give Alpha my all. I was hungry for the brotherhood, history, poems, servitude, and life lessons. But my soul was not for sale.

Many months passed until spring of my senior year arrived, and I could finally unmask myself before an anxious crowd at our "probate,"[46] with a bald head and black-n'-gold face paint, to declare myself—along with my two other "line brothers"—an Alpha man. I stood alongside Thomas, the most popular kid on campus who would follow me a year later as commencement speaker himself; and Damola, a scholarship-earning walk-on running back, business

---

46 The unveiling ceremony of new fraternity of sorority initiates to the public.

student turned tech-star, and a Nigerian immigrant on a mission, though never too busy to be there when it counted: my father's passing, my *katb al-kitab*[47] party in Dearborn, and on FaceTime months later when my wife Malak and I had a village-style wedding outside her family's east side home during the COVID-19 pandemic.

The bruhs showed up in droves for my college graduation, interrupting my commencement speech when I shouted them out, to holler our call-and-response from the theatre balcony: "One! One! One! One! One! One! *Nnnnniiiiiiiinnnnneeeee!*"

"Oooooooooooo-Six!"

"A-*Phiiiiiiiiiii!*"

"A!"

I chuckled awkwardly, hoping it wouldn't mess up my memorized speech. Afterward, I tensed up again when brothers formed a large circle around me on the stairs of Northrup Auditorium. I was anxious at what Baba may be thinking about my being in a fraternity and about our ceremonious traditions as each brother crossed his arms across the front of his body and used his pinky fingers to link up with brothers standing on his left and right. We all began with a loud baritone *hummm* before singing our Alpha hymn. When it was all sung and done, I looked up at Baba, who was beaming with pride. "Now I understand why you joined this group," he said smiling.

Unlike most fraternities, whose memberships typically expired after college, Alpha was a lifelong brotherhood. As part

---

47 Islamic marriage ceremony. Literal translation: signing/writing of the contract/book.

of the "Divine Nine"—a reference to the oldest, historically Black fraternities and sororities—we prided ourselves on academic achievement, career success, and community service. And though I barely had a moment to soak up "A Phi A" on campus, I continued to soak up its blessings beyond it, like when I graduated and interviewed with Clarksdale High as a new Teach for America Corps Member and discovered that my interviewer was a sister of Alpha Kappa Alpha, our sister sorority. I played to that privilege as I pleaded:

"Soror,[48] there's *dozens* of TFA Corps Members who wanna be here. You gotta fight for me, please."

"You don't even worry, brother Ali," she said.

Or my principal at Clarksdale High, a "Zeta"[49] who named me "Mr. Ali" and always quoted her Bible to remind me, "You have not because you ask not, Mr. Ali."[50] Or brother Dowling whom I met in Detroit and who wrote me a letter of recommendation to help me jump off my MBA waitlist into Emory University, where another Alpha brother, who happened to be the dean, felt inspired by my application. I knew this much because Dean Brian—who I presume was at least partly moved by my commitment to A Phi A—complimented my application on the first day we met and pulled me in to exchange our Alpha grip.[51] He then gave me a powerful dean's push with a letter

---

48   Sister (in this context, a member of a sister-sorority).

49   Zeta Phi Beta Sorority, Incorporated—one of the "Divine Nine."

50   The end of the Biblical verse James 4:2: "You do not have, because you do not ask God."

51   Term for a secret handshake exchanged by members of the same fraternity or sorority.

of rec for Harvard, where, after being admitted, my doctoral advisor Dr. Deborah Jewell-Sherman—who was married to a now-late Alpha man—became a mother-like figure.

Then there was that Alpha brother I met just once when I was at Harvard. He was a graduate student nearby at MIT whose campus I visited one day to attend an Alpha Phi Alpha probate. I stood there sporting my crossing jacket, watching with nostalgia as initiates crossed "the burning sands" into our brotherhood. It was a sunny and beautiful evening, and I was relishing my escape from the 100-plus pages left to read before the next morning, in true Harvard fashion. But this buff brother stole my happy moment with a hungry stare into my soul, a stare I noticed from a distance and monitored from my periphery, until I stared back to let him know it was either love or it was "on." It became the first staring match with my own brother in six years as an Alpha—six years in which I had grown a lot, though not out of my Fordson boy, and I was still willing to risk whatever to prove it.

"Sup, *bruh*?!" I yelled.

I nodded my head upward in his direction, across a crowd of twenty feet, somewhat aggressively, but followed with a smirk to suggest there was still time for him to salvage our unborn relationship, despite whatever preconceived notions he had.

My "sup" seemed to satisfy his search, or awaken him from it, and as he walked over to me, I sensed he was a kindred spirit.

"I'm sorry, brother, I don't know why I was staring at you

like that," he said.

"All good, my brother," I said, smiling back as we hugged and gripped.

Perhaps my pale white skin provoked his suspicion that I somehow paid my way into Alpha without enduring the sweat and tears of initiation.

He asked where I was from and what I did. I barely spoke a few sentences about Harvard and music before he said, "You know Young Guru?"

"Oh yeah, I do."

I only vaguely recognized the name, but I googled him right after to learn he was the famous mix engineer behind the sound of Jay-Z.

"I met his manager the other day, Jerald Cooper," he said. "He told me to keep my eye out for someone like you, bruh, a smart, education kid, big on hip-hop. I'mma give you his number. He's looking for you."

That was Tuesday, and by Thursday I'd play hooky[52] at Harvard and stroll my way to the Amtrak where I rode a few hours into New York City to meet with Jerald and Guru. We sat in the booth behind baseball hall-of-famer Derek Jeter at the SoHo House in Manhattan. SoHo became our regular meet spot when we weren't dashing through the city in an Uber to meet with a PR firm or grab food, as Guru dazzled me with fun facts like how many unreleased Prince tracks lived on his hard drive; or how Live Nation's business model disrupted the music industry; and how excited he and 9th Wonder were for

---

52 Skip class. Fordson prepped me well—at least for that part.

their new artist Rapsody on Jamla Records, and their soon-to-be-inked deal with Roc Nation, which Live Nation owned.

Just a month later I was back at MIT, moving with Guru through crowds who stood eagerly and starry-eyed, awaiting his wisdom on the future of music and tech. We grabbed late-night pizza after a long day of stops and events across the city. It was during this visit—and through Jerald's connects—that I met the folks who would later hire me to work for Live Nation during the last year of my doctoral program. Months later, from Hollywood, I was flown out on Live Nation's dollar to attend the *Made in America Fest,* where I sat next to Jay-Z's mom in Roc Nation's VIP tent as Beyoncé prepared to perform.

Just like that, my thirst to be accepted, and my determination to climb, brought me within one degree of Jay-Z, Alicia Keys, Beyoncé, and the other hip-hop legends whose music was engineered by Young Guru. So close, and so lost, 'cause I was searching for purpose in the material world, in fame, while unbeknownst to me, Prophet Muhammad (s) had warned: "Being famous suffices to make a man a sinner, for good fame makes him slip—unless the Exalted God showers His mercy on him—and bad fame brings him evil." I was, as many-a-Holy-Prophet-and-Imam narrate, "drinking from a salt sea." The more of the world I drank, the thirstier—and more delusional—I became.

"Fearlessly and boldly help truth and justice. Bear patiently the sufferings and face bravely the obstacles which come in your way when you follow the truth and when you try to uphold it. Adhere to the cause of truth and justice, wherever you find it."

-Imam Ali ibn Abi Taleb (as)

10. RETIRED

I was hoping my five-hour flight from Detroit to San Francisco would offer a mental break from the countless lawsuits and complaints, now arriving on seemingly a weekly basis. But just before boarding my flight, I couldn't block out the calls I received from my counseling secretary and Mr. Ralph, the director of human resources at DPS. As I listened to Mr. Ralph search far and wide for words to justify yet another investigation, I recalled an email I had sent him more than a year prior—clearly in vain.

> August 13, 2008
>
> Dear [Mr. Ralph]:
>
> This is not the first time I respond to such allegations directed toward my honesty, integrity, and character as a whole. Last year I spent an hour and forty minutes in a closed session meeting with the entire Board of Education responding to the same allegations.
>
> You informed me during our meeting on Friday, August 8, 2008, that [Ms. Dalilah] filed a complaint with the ADSA president, which was submitted later to

the superintendent. [Ms. Dalilah] alleges that close to seventy students from Fordson High School graduated short of the required credits or did not meet the graduation requirements at Fordson in 2005, 2006 and 2007.

Attached to this letter is a detailed response to each of the transcripts. I do acknowledge on four transcripts the students graduated without a required class such as World Civics I or World Civics II. I will review the procedure my counselors and administrative staff follow to prevent any such oversights in the future.

[However], I draw your attention to the DFT contract (page 10, line 4): "*the determination of credit or non-credit shall be the responsibility of the administration.*" If the principal is granted this authority and he or she exercises this option for legitimate reasons, I do not see any merit for this complaint.

Furthermore, I do believe that [Ms. Dalilah] is in clear and direct violation of the FERPA Act. When she accessed students' transcripts, on February 28, 2008, and March 3, 2008, she was assigned to a different building and she should not have accessed students' private records without parental consent.

As a building administrator, I am granted access to other high schools and middle schools in the district; and yet, under no circumstances would I access transcripts from other buildings for any reason, without prior authorization from the building principal and/or parents or students.

Finally, it is my belief that [Ms. Dalilah] is being vindictive and I would ask that the paper she wrote be placed in her personnel file to be reviewed, to fully comprehend her motives.

In the past four years, I have been investigated more than ten times, most of which were based on anonymous tips to the school board or to the super-intendent. I would hope that this school year, I will be given the opportunity to concentrate on teaching and learning and meeting *Adequate Yearly Progress.*

With Dr. Artis now retired, my support system had grown weaker. Settling into my hotel room, I washed up, performed *wudu*,[53] prayed, grabbed a cup of coffee, and opened my laptop to write an email to my new superintendent, Mr. Whiston.

Good day:

Just arrived to San Francisco. This morning, prior to my departure, I received a call from [Mr. Ralph]. He informed me that he will be conducting an investiga-tion and talking to employees and staff members. He would not elaborate or give me any idea about who, what, where...and he asked me not to speak to anyone regarding this matter.

About an hour later, my counseling secretary called to notify me about a call she received from HR re-garding an investigation. HR would like to interview

---

53 Ablution. A purification ritual in Islam (typically in preparation for *salah,* or prayer).

her regarding a "sexual harassment investigation" and she asked me if she should talk to them with or without union representation. I told her, "If it makes you comfortable, have union representation, talk to [Mr. Ralph], and tell him everything you know. [Ralph] is a straight shooter." End of conversation.

I am afraid that I have become an easy target and my civility has been mistaken for weakness [and wrongfulness]… A handful of teachers filed a complaint with the Dearborn Federation of Teachers [DFT] about a hostile work environment. The complaint was given to the superintendent, and he gave it to the Michigan Leadership Institute [MLI] members. Up until this date, despite asking several times myself and despite formal requests from my union president, the MLI won't give me a copy. I asked to at least be made aware of what I have been accused of…they refused.

I will be back early Friday morning and [Mr. Ralph] would like to interview me next week. Please be assured to the maximum extent that I have no skeletons in my closet. As a matter of fact, it is very clean: personally, academically, and professionally.

Imad Fadlallah

Exercising my right under the Freedom of Information Act to obtain a copy of the complaint availed me nothing. Eventually, I had to spend thousands of dollars to retain an attorney and wait several months to procure the DFT document that formalized numerous complaints about me.

Meanwhile, the investigation by the MLI—which included the Institute examining every keystroke ever made on my keyboard—failed to yield the results my enemy faction was hoping for. Despite this faction handpicking the MLI for their cause and priming the investigation with alarming allegations, the Institute ultimately recommended that I stay put, with better support around me.

However, even with the MLI's vote of confidence, the Institute was far from objective, for its biases and unconscious bigotry bled through many of the forty-four pages and forty recommendations made to the district. Excerpts from this *Detroit News* article summarized one of them this way:

> A recommendation to bar Arabic speech in the city's most heavily Arab public high school unless it is absolutely necessary has sparked a sharp debate between those who say it's necessary to help students perform better and those who say it only helps alienate them.
>
> A study commissioned by the Wayne County Regional Education Service Agency said the use of Arabic by students in the bilingual programs in Dearborn Public Schools slows the assimilation of students "into the school and American society in general" and fosters suspicion among students and teachers who don't speak the language.
>
> The 44-page report from the Michigan Leadership Institute, an independent education and municipal consulting group based in Old Mission in the Grand Traverse Bay area...took note of the specific challenges

for the district with an Arab population that reaches as high as 90 percent in some schools.

"To do otherwise reinforces a perception by some that Fordson is an Arab School in America rather than an American school with Arab students," the report stated.

District officials said they will explore ways to accelerate students into English-only classes over the next 18 months.

Intissar Harajli, the district's coordinator of bilingual education, said the district tests all new students' English proficiency and places them in English-only or bilingual classes according to their skill level. All schools and all subjects have bilingual options.

"The misconception is sometimes (determining) when the child has [enough] survival skills [to] move on," Harajli said, adding that it [can] take up to four years for a new English speaker to gain the skills to adapt to an English-only classroom.

[Kurt Kline], president of the Dearborn Federation of Teachers and a former economics teacher at Fordson, said a bilingual education is necessary in the school district, home to many students and parents who are new to the English language. Yet, he agreed with the report's assessment that the use of languages other than English "contributes to an atmosphere of distrust and suspicion on the part of English-only speaking adults in the schools."

"The report's concern is that there's an overuse of the native tongue when there doesn't really need to be," [Kline] said. When English speakers choose to communicate in Arabic, he said, "It does make me suspicious, and I think it's rude for them to do this. If situations were reversed, how would you feel? I don't think they get that."[54]

The MLI recommendation right before this one suggested that our district evaluate the practices of other districts that adapted well to changing demographics. The irony is this: the districts they recommended we take notes from were developing dual-language immersion programs[55] and embracing the language, culture, and identity of their students to promote

---

54   It appears this article, published in 2009 by Tanveer Ali, was removed from the web. Fortunately, we have a copy preserved on our drive. Nevertheless, numerous texts reference the quotes discussed in this article. For example, in their 2012 book, "Education and Capitalism: Struggles for Learning and Liberation," Jeff Bale and Sarah Knopp use the quote about Arabic reinforcing "a perception by some that Fordson is an Arab school" as evidence for this statement: "...the anti-immigrant backlash since the 1970s has led to specific policies that have outlawed bilingual education. At times, the bigots behind this backlash have used attacks on bilingual education to inch their cause into the political mainstream... at the same time, a decade of war and occupation has poisoned the political climate for Arab and Muslim Americans in particular, but also for *any* group hoping to use school to maintain the home language and culture."

55   A form of education or curriculum in which teachers utilize both languages—in this case, English and Arabic—to help students build literacy and climb a steep learning curve. Research shows that this approach is optimal for English Language Learners (ELLs).

overall literacy, education, and mental health. The studies on this topic, often centering on English-Spanish programs, demonstrate that this approach does not come at the expense of learning English; rather, it accelerates this process for English Language Learners (ELLs) like those in Dearborn Public Schools, while fostering a caring, inclusive, and personalized learning environment. And yet the MLI—a practically all-White firm from Traverse City with no claim to expertise in teaching or reaching multilingual and multicultural groups—insisted that it knew where to start: minimizing Arabic to minimize suspicion.

In 2008, after a courageous career as superintendent, Dr. John Artis retired and began teaching at U of M – Dearborn. Just prior to Dr. Artis' retirement, DFT President Kurt Kline pointed to the chair in my office and told my assistant principal, Mrs. Sizzle, "I'll be sitting there next year. And you won't be here." I was later informed that the school board president guaranteed Kline that Kline would replace me in my role as Fordson's principal—on the condition that he would help a new superintendent take the helm. Kline, who also served on the committee that prepared the interview questions for superintendency, bragged about coaching the new superintendent the night before his interview. By Kline's admission, this was done with the expectation that the school board president—

and the new superintendent—would "return the favor." Thus, Dr. Artis was succeeded by a superintendent who was hired through a biased process that involved collusion from within the hiring committee.

So, this was the story of my professional life at Fordson High: dealing with biased policies, bigoted leaders, and a building that was at least ten years behind. I wish I was hopeful that by the time a new generation reads this, this gap will have closed any amount—but I must admit I am skeptical, at best, about that possibility. For so long as the roots of bigotry remain alive and strong within our city and district—and so long as our parents and families remain largely unaware of these realities—this gap will only widen. And Fordson High will remain, as I told Dr. John Artis, a prison—of young minds.

"Allah gave angels intellect without desire. He gave animals desire without intellect. And He gave the human being both. Thus, the human who lets their intellect reign over their desire is superior to an angel. While the one who lets their desire reign over their intellect is inferior to an animal."

-Imam Ali ibn Abi Taleb (as)

11. DELUSIONAL

"Mississippi Blues"

It's just you and an occasional flock of birds for miles upon Mississippi miles, on a skinny two-lane highway surrounded by vast cornfields, when suddenly a brassy drone, half the size of a helicopter, swoops down to car level and you realize you're going to die. *Chill,* you think. *It's called a crop duster, remember?* Your heart rate begins to recover. Your hands quit choking the wheel. Your fears surrender with the sun to Mississippi's hopeful gold moon.

It's your third visit back to the Birthplace of the Blues since leaving your classroom in Clarksdale. Highway 61's tall wheats wave peacefully in the mild wind to welcome you, a generous contrast to the stern, prickly cotton plants that rarely flinch. You cross Highway 49, the famous intersection where Robert Johnson sold his soul to the devil in exchange for mastery of the blues… so the tale goes. It's a few degrees below hell. Juke Joint weekend. The Blues Fest. You're back in the land of flying cockroaches. Live musicians. Carts selling fried Kool-Aid pickles and elephant ears. A large truck hauling sheep, dogs, and monkeys sits in an open field, and you'd never imagine why. First, someone tells you, and you don't believe them. Minutes later, you watch awestruck as the dispirited monkeys hop like horsemen onto the obedient, tail-wagging dogs. The shepherd dogs begin herding the compliant sheep in a large, speeding circle.

Now you're so bewildered you call your best-teacher-friend: "Bro, you gotta come see this sh**; they got a monkeys riding dogs herding sheep show." Thirty minutes later you stand there with him—your ACT-prep partner. He was the math to your literacy. You're proud that you shared students. You're excited to share a visit, a new story. Down the block stands one of America's lowest academically achieving high schools. And middle schools. And elementary schools. A curious sheep struts astray.

You stroll around the festival, basking in the blues and your local fame. You spot your ex-student Napoleon. Approaching him, you yell, "OH! SO! Napolo!" in honor of his Twitter handle, and your endorphins erupt, swimming inside like a pack of happy dolphins. You prep your abs because he's the funniest kid in the South. Not tonight. His face reads: T-R-A-G-E-D-Y.

You don't admit it, but you know that last visit was your last visit. Back home in Michigan, your ex-student Junior comes to mind, and you text him. Turns out he's visiting family nearby. You invite him to spend the night in your music studio and now you're both there, toggling between talk about gang life and the music industry.

"Man, I love Pac," he says.

"You know what Pac said, right?" you say eagerly. "'I'm not sayin' I'm gonna change the world, but I *guarantee you* I'll spark the brain that will!' He was talking about you, Junior."

His brown cheeks redden as he smirks shyly, nodding, and then raising his gaze with conviction. He asks like he's mustered up months of courage:

"Why you stop teaching, Mr. Ali?"

You collect yourself. "I loved the classroom. Love Clarksdale. Love y'all, man. But how much time did I have in your mind? Hour during class, hour after? Then what? You were bangin'? But Gucci Mane, Nicki Minaj, Yo Gotti... they really had you, right?

"I left 'cause I need more time in your mind, Junior. We need real music on the radio, role models in our streets, culture in our curriculum. I'm busy with that." Next thing you know, you're rapping for him over a piano-driven hip-hop track. It's the song you never shared; it's Buddy's song.

> Was excited to see Buddy over at the Blues Fest
> Memories make my heart
> Thump-thump through my chest
> I guess we need deaths to inspire more Blues?
> If you could see the I.C.U.; hallway all full
> People like me n' you
> Watchin' the end of Kenneth Jr., how sad
> Clarksdale: where juniors can't outlive dad

T-R-A-G-E-D-Y. You stare square at Napolean and the dolphins disappear like water down a drain.

"They got Buddy, Mr. Ali."

You stand in the well-lit festival in a dark daze. That's all he knows: the other gang shot. Buddy's dead. Seven hours pass, and Brittannica calls: "Mr. Ali, Buddy still alive! My ni**a a soldier." She follows firmly, voice raised: "Bruh ain't goin' nowhere!"

Junior's eyes water. He's built like a middleweight boxer. If you had to choose one of your 360 students whose walls you couldn't break, you'd choose Junior. You watch them crumble as you continue:

> Shared his dreams with me too, eyes grew:
> "Mr. Ali, I'm a mechanic; I love cars!
> I love fixing cars, n' I'm really good at it
> I'll fix yours if it's damaged
> Wanna study cars in college if I can manage."
> Remember smiling at em'
> "Buddy, I'm with you every step of the way!"
> What a way our steps ended that Saturday

T-R-A-G-E-D-Y. You hang up with Brittannica and hit Highway 61 in a dash to Memphis Hospital. You keep trying to block out the anger. You fail. *Seventy ******* miles and across state lines to get treated?*

His mother hovers over him, possessed in prayer. You stand around his swollen head with the others, cheerleading in silence. The doctor steps in to pronounce Buddy brain-dead. You return the rental and catch a flight to Detroit.

It's been a year, but today, Junior is in Michigan mourning Buddy in your studio. Now you want him baptized in his own tears:

> Act like you're destined for these streets
> And they'll invite you
> Stray dogs will bite you; street cats will fight you
> Gang-lords will hype you
> Tell you that you're "next"
> Next what? Death? 'Cause you sent the wrong text?
> Play tough young blood, til a bullet's in your face
> Would you rather swallow pride
> Or learn how swallowed-bullets taste?

Shameless streams run down Junior's face. Instead of tissues, you offer him the mic. He records a five-minute freestyle, his soul spilled free, collected on CD. Gang life. Abuse. Poor education. He takes it back to Clarksdale where your many ex-students spend summer picking prickly cotton for less than minimum wage. It dawns on you: *My God, isn't that a slave?*

Maybe he'll share his song. Maybe it'll start a revolution.

It wasn't what I expected for my very first days at Harvard—to write "Mississippi Blues," a short story that Harvard's ALA-NA Anthology would soon publish. But I was grateful for Dr. Nancy Sommers' creative nonfiction workshop that created mental space for me to reflect on those two transformative years after college, when I poured into boys and girls who held a mirror to me, reflecting back my lack of self-love, the toxic marriage to media and music that still consumed my days, the lethargy with literacy I still wrestled with, and how lost I truly was despite my assignment to help lead their way.

> Where I taught, schools fail, but you learn a lot
> Pain makes you wise, see, my kids hurt a lot
> Talkin' Mississippi, now, I'm sure you heard a lot
> 'Cause Mississippi's a movie America don't care to watch
> *-I'll Be Me, 2013*

I recall those Mississippi days vividly, like that night after I had just turned twenty-one and the wrong way on that same, secluded two-lane highway, realizing immediately, but not fast enough to avoid the flashing sirens of the state sheriff hiding on the highway's shoulder who couldn't have expected *that* stupid of a scene to unfold before him on a late Sunday night, when I was driving home half-asleep, as if attempting career and life suicide altogether.

Before requesting my license and registration, he asked what the hell was wrong with me, and whether I was intoxicated. "No sir," I said, flashing my teacher's badge and pleading with him in my exquisite White voice, explaining that I was a new eleventh-grade teacher at Clarksdale High just trying to get home after a long night of planning lessons for my students, who I had to wake up for at 6:30 a.m. I pointed to my GPS to show I was just minutes from home. Apparently, I made a coherent-enough case that he thought it over, and in a rare stroke of fortune with five-o, he decided to let me go.

But that night was no wakeup call, for that wouldn't arrive until months later on the morning I awoke on that same highway shoulder after running into a Clarksdale barber whom I knew at a party in Cleveland, Mississippi, and he offered me something that had me pondering for the few moments it laid there in my palm—*why? What's wrong? Why am I so much more willing than others to be reckless with my body and life?*

Later that night, I put my car in drive and fell asleep behind the wheel where I woke up to the sound of my tires running over the rumble stripes on the shoulder as my Nissan Altima veered off toward the cornfields. Once I regained control, I shifted into park and fell asleep, awakening hours later to my engine still on and no policeman to be found, feeling grateful to the God I had forgotten, before I continued thirty minutes north on 61 toward the safety of my home.

As pretty of a ranch as it was for $999 a month, split three-ways between my boys Tosh and John, 504 W. 2nd St. wasn't as safe as we had hoped. And, in a strange way, it seemed that each scary event—the drunk driver who nosedived into my Altima at 4 a.m., completely destroying it, or the one student who never showed up to class but showed up to my home to shoot a BB gun through my car, or the students I didn't even teach who threw a brick through my home window, or the countless gunshots heard through the night—were the exact reminders I needed that I wasn't as invincible as I thought I was.

But as a 26-year-old at Harvard, I was somewhat of a new man, a journey that began almost three years prior when I committed to being clean. I was, at least for two years at that point, praying my five daily prayers. I was humbled. But the reform was just beginning.

> I don't "stunt" 'cause that would stunt my growth
> I quit blunts in 2012 it wasn't 'cause my throat
> Medic said, "Don't panic, you're manic
> 'Cause weed's a psychedelic."
> When you smoke it stunts your growth, *cuz*—
> Yeah, I said it!
>> *-Reach Beyond, 2019*

My heart raced as I phoned Harvard's Counseling and Mental Health Services office that fall in 2014. The fear—at least from my perspective—was very real: maybe I'd jeopardize my dream-come-true, my fully-funded doctoral program, if I shared too much and they determined I was mentally unfit for schooling. But as I left Harvard's Yard to cross Mass Avenue onto Holyoke Street where I lived, the sweet voice of the elderly woman on the other line brought me a temporary calm: "What makes you reach out today, Ali?"

"Uh... I'm a doctoral student here, and uh, I've previously suffered from a manic episode, uh, about three years back, and I feel like I'm still dealing with a lot of repercussions, uh, from it, so I'm just wondering if uh, there are any therapists in-house you would, you know, recommend?"

She asked several more probing questions, *mmming* and *yessing* as she studied my words, before concluding, "Yes, I understand... you know, Ali, you *could* see one of our therapists, but your story makes me think about someone who I believe would be a great fit for you. He practices psychodynamic therapy."

> His name is Brent / my therapist
> Pay him like rent to stare at *this*
> -*Lessons from Grief, 2019*

My first thought was that "Brent" sounded super White, and I can't say I was thrilled when I pulled up the picture of him on *Psychology Today* and confirmed as much. But on second glance, he had a kind and friendly face that gave me a good vibe, and I decided to give him a try. After several sessions, I felt at ease—psychologically safe, as they love to say at Harvard—especially when he studied my words for days on end before affirming, "I understand why you want to be here, Ali. I just want to say that. And I'm glad you are."

That was perhaps the moment I handed him the key and asked God to free me from my mental prison by letting Brent help shine a light through its dark underground tunnels and reveal my escape route. So, the work began. I would later rap about it in a song I released in 2019, after Baba's passing, with lyrics that help summarize some of my first conversations with Brent as I recounted the events of my manic episode in 2012 and the delusions that followed:

> This was that time when I lost it
> Baba waits back in the car; he's exhausted
> I'm in the stu, recording a song
> He cries to Allah, "Tell me where I went wrong?"
> He says, "Pop it in"
> "No, I won't play it"
> "Oh yes, you will; I'll hear what you're sayin"
> He listens close; he tells me it's weak
> I can't even speak; been makin' him weep
> Ironic, tears only make 'em look stronger
> "You're rushing your songs; they should all take you longer"
> I'm hurt; but shocked that he gave it his ears
> Acknowledging his—and my—biggest fear
> That my career won't look like my brother's
> I seek validation and mercy from mother
> "Be happy," she tells me, "but please in another

Form;" Mama, for this I was born
Baba, for this I was born
Oh, how I dove in those waters within
Bleeding from sin, healing to swim
Nearly I drowned, once and again
Insurmountable pressure to win
Mama, I pray these words illuminate it
Status quo bowed when your child disobeyed it
I'm Allah's maid so forever I made it
Clean lines of mine would make Baba elated
-Lessons from Grief, 2019

For over five years, between 2014 and 2020, I met with Brent weekly, reliving each day of each trauma. During the nights after my sessions, I sat in silence to reflect, allowing the guilt for who I had become to wash over me, and reliving dark moments to sit with them instead of shoving them back into my subconscious. Yet during the daytime, as my knowledge in adult psychology grew by way of Harvard's classrooms, I was helping to lead the way for others again, this time as a teaching assistant for graduate students from across campus, as I led my own section of Dr. Kegan's famous *Adult Development* course. The irony wasn't lost on me: I was helping students identify mental roadblocks and overcome them with success, much like I did in Mississippi—all while I suffered with my own mental illness.

I felt blessed to have new theories and tools to support my journey, especially ones that aligned with what Islam was teaching me: that reconciling with one's self can't only be about regret; rather, self-reconciliation must also include empathy and be free of unproductive shaming, so that we are best positioned to diagnose the sources of our brokenness. And therefore, best positioned to heal.

As Brent put it in one session, "That's the paradox, Ali, that by leaning into the problem it offers you more relief than running from it." And so, there was no other route than to revisit the traumas that had brought me to therapy and all the pain I created along the way, both for myself and others. And except for Mama, nobody was more devastated by *shaytaan's* grasp on me as Baba was. I knew this not only from the tears and torment I witnessed on his face during my lowest moments, but also from his letters, ones he wrote me while I was mentally ill. And like letters to an inmate, they were few and far in between. But they always had my undivided attention, even when the devil was doing his best work to distract me.

The Prison Letters

It was 2010 when Baba wrote me his first letter. I can't recall what I said to prompt it, but I know his email was a response to a request of mine, for I was in a deep search for answers. I was thirsty for a stronger sense of identity, belonging, Islam— though I was far from ready to embrace it. Perhaps Baba also suspected that I was losing my way, though he was, I knew, proud of me at the time—partly because he was unaware of my hidden habits in his absence.

What he knew, for the most part, was that the kid who was bailed out of a holding cell four years prior had just delivered a college commencement speech in front of 4,000-plus attendees before joining the Teach for America Corps. Baba had just visited Clarksdale, Mississippi and spent several days observing my instruction, giving me feedback, and mentoring me through my first days as a teacher.

But at minimum, I'm fairly certain he also knew that his children had fallen at least somewhat victim to America's toxic machine of media, anti-Arabism, Islamophobia, hyper-sexualization, and many other corrupt Western ideals, and that he had underestimated this machine as well as his role in combatting it. I suspect that he believed his purity and prayers, his piousness and principles, would be enough to shield us from the poison of the world. *I don't have to preach what I practice...* I imagine he thought. And by the time he realized he *did* have to talk his talk, and not just walk his walk, I was lost.

Baba began late one Friday night on February 19, 2010—six months into my first year as a teacher—by reintroducing himself, perhaps to help me know who *I* am. The subject of his email read "As promised" and contained one line: "Please read carefully with an open mind." Attached was a Microsoft Word document that began as follows.

Dear Ali:

As promised, I will start this journey...

My name is Imad Fadlallah, my father's name is

Mahmoud, and my grandfather is Asaad. My great grandfather is Fadlallah, and his father is Ali, and his father is Nisrallah, and his father is Ali, and his father is Youssuf, and his father is Youssuf, and his father is Mohammed, and his father is Fadlallah, and his father is Mohammad, and his father is Mohammad, and his father is Youssuf, and his father is Badreddine, and his father is Ali, and his father is Mohammad, and his father is Jaafar, and his father is Youssuf, and his father is Mohammad, and his father is Hassan, and his father is Issa, and his father is Fadel, and his father is Yehya, and his father is Jouban, and his father is Alhassan, and his father is Diab, and his father is Abdullah, and his father is Mohammad, and his father is Yehya, and his father is Mohammad, and his father is Dawood, and his father is Idris, and his father is Dawood, and his father is Ahmad, and his father is Abdallah, and his father is Moussa, and his father is Abdallah, and his father is Alhassan, and his father is Alhassan ibn Ali (as), and his father is Ali ibn Abi Taleb (as).

Imam Ali (as) was married to Fatimah (as), the daughter of Prophet Muhammad (s). We are descendants from his oldest son Imam Hassan (as). Sayid Muhsen Alamine, a scholar in South Lebanon in the early 19th century said in his book about the villages and towns of Jabal Amel (the geographical region south and east of Saida) about Ainata: " ...and to it moved from Mecca the honorable Fadlallahs, descendants of Imam Hassan (as), son of Imam Ali (as), and they are a house of knowledge and wisdom…"

Prophet Muhammad (s) said, "I am the city of knowledge and Ali is its gate." I will start this conversation with a letter Imam Ali (as) wrote to Malik Al-Ashtar when he made him Governor of Egypt. The reason I picked this letter is because it highlights several of Imam Ali (as)'s philosophies in governance, jurisprudence, and human rights. I beg of you to read the letter carefully hoping that you do not skip a word. In brief, this can be the start of a constitution.

Something changed in me when I read those first two paragraphs. I felt the significance I was searching for—seen in a true way—perhaps for the first time in my adult life. Maybe deep in my subconscious I also felt shame that I wasn't prepared to confront. I skimmed the Holy Imam's letter to Malik Al-Ashtar, one of the most noble companions of the Holy Prophet (s) and his Progeny (as). I found inspiration and comfort in the divine letter, but also found it a bit dense and beyond the scope of thinking I was prepared to embrace. I assigned some sort of grandiosity to Prophet Muhammad (s) and his Holy Progeny (as) who guided Baba's values, but they were no heroes in my life. How could they be when I had no real idea who they were? I had just dove deeper, for example, into the world of Bob Marley, and that seemed more up my alley.

It would be more than two years before the letters continued, except for occasional notes Baba dropped to me when he escaped to his sanctuary—the home he built atop a mountain in Qulaile, where he would soon be buried.

> Imad <email redacted>
> Mon, Dec 27, 2010, 4:35 PM
> to Ali
> جنوبي الهوى قلبي وما أحلاه أن يغدو هوى قلبي جنوبيا
> You asked if I am in the *jnoub*.[56] I replied with poetry.
> The South is the love of my heart, and how beautiful it
> is for my loving heart to become from the South.
> Imad Fadlallah

> Imad <email redacted>
> Mon, Dec 27, 2010, 5:05 PM
> to Ali
> It is midnight in Qulaile. The wind speed outside ex-
> ceeds 60 mph. The shutters are about to explode, and
> the brick tiles on the roof are dancing up and down. It
> sounds like a jumbo jet flying at a low altitude. On the
> way home around 11pm I encountered a fox crossing
> in front of the gate. No rain yet—just high wind. I love it.
> Imad Fadlallah

He loved it, indeed; but his sanctuary time was always short-
lived. And away from it, Baba was buried in lawsuits, all while
fathering thousands more children as he faced the end of his
road as a revolutionary principal—for only five full years—at
Fordson High.

Plus, I wasn't the only one writing to him, so to speak, or

---

56 South.

the only one he was busy writing back to. I was just one inmate in the seemingly endless maze of prison cells that were lined up like hallway lockers in our Dearborn Public Schools. And Fordson kids were just a fraction of the thousands more he worked day and night to help free.

There was, for example, Asia Mohamed, who arrived as a new immigrant in 1999 and enrolled in eighth grade at Stout Middle School:

> "I felt isolated and afraid. I couldn't speak English and was unable to make friends. Since I didn't participate in gym, I often found myself in the principal's office. One day, Mr. Fadlallah asked me about my hobbies, and I shared my love for writing Arabic poetry. He left and returned with a journal filled with his own, handwritten Arabic poems that he shared with me. I still have a copy of his handwriting. His words of encouragement and shared interest in poetry gave me hope. When I moved to high school, my next principal pulled me aside for not participating in gym and specifically told me, 'You will never receive a high school diploma… you are destined to fail, Asia.' Today, years later, as I near the completion of my doctorate in education at U of M, I often reflect back on both principals: the one who believed in me and my talents, and the other who dismissed them. I'm forever grateful for Mr. Fadlallah."

And when it wasn't Asia, it was Alicia "Lily" Bernard one year later, in 2000, one of Stout's leading problem-childs:

"I was a troubled young girl who was always down on herself. But Mr. Fadlallah didn't see it that way. He saw something in me. He went above and beyond to help me even though it took many years to recognize what his words and actions meant. When I kept getting in trouble, he took me on a daytrip, just me and him, to visit Vista Maria for a tour—a transitional living facility for 'vulnerable youth.' He figured, 'Let me show her where she'll end up if she keeps down this path.' At first, I was excited—he drove a white Mercedes at the time, and I thought I just wanted to ride in his cool car. But when we were there, he left me in the bathroom with some of the girls to get a taste of what it's like. They were scrubbing the bathroom floor. It was terrifying—and I realized I jumped the gun on this one!"

Afterward, Baba treated Lily to McDonald's, knowing her first-hand experience was a sufficient teacher.

And when it wasn't Lily, it was Adnan Kattan, who arrived at Stout six months after landing in Detroit from Lebanon in 2001 and assembled one of the thickest files of write-ups and teacher complaints that ever lived on Baba's desk:

"Kids would try to bully me for my accent or whatever, so I kept fighting—cafeterias, classrooms, the bus, locker room, everywhere. I had a 1.4 GPA and Mr. Fadlallah was fed up. One day, I did something *very* stupid, call it 'an act of indecency,' and I could've been expelled, or worse. When Mr. Fadlallah called me into the office, a Dearborn police officer was there. Mr. Fadlallah told me to sit down and held his thumb and pointer finger a half-inch apart before yelling at me: 'I'm *this close* to taking this file, and you, and tossing you both outta' this building and onto that street for good! You understand me!?' He began asking the officer about all the possible punishments for what I did. Juvenile jail was on the table. I was terrified. Then he pointed at the officer's handcuffs and said, 'Decision time, Adnan. You wanna leave with him or stay with me!?' I wanted to straighten my act, but I felt it was too late because my father was even more fed up than Mr. Fadlallah, and if he told him, I was 100% heading back to Lebanon. Mr. Fadlallah had a good relationship with my parents, so he knew this, and decided not to tell them. I couldn't believe it. But he kept constant tabs on me and kept me in check. I was part of the class that followed him to Fordson. I watched him transform it from chaos to a real school. He was more hands-on than people will ever know: fixing our schedules or calling colleges when counselors shooed us away, negotiating with everyone on our behalf. I became a 4.2 student—and he would smile at my report cards like the proud, second father that he was. Not just to me but hundreds of us—no matter where you came from."

It continued this way, child after child, year after year at Stout and Fordson—where Baba even went after students who were expelled from Dearborn Public Schools, like Mohammad Tiba, the menace to society turned maven for good, whom Baba somehow managed to reinstate at Fordson, on the condition that Tiba would attend all PTA meetings where he used the same internet savvy that got him expelled to coach parents and teachers on internet safety. Despite his transformation from a 0.6 GPA sixth grader at Stout, to a 3.75 GPA senior at Fordson, Tiba was told by an administrator that he could not attend the Class of '06 graduation ceremony, given his likelihood of pulling a final stunt on the big stage. Baba overruled the decision; and on graduation day, after Mr. Fadlallah announced his name, Tiba marched forth resolutely before suddenly unzipping his gown and turning toward the bleachers to reveal his t-shirt that read, "Happy Birthday, Mom!" He reflected on the moment with the following:

> "While handing my diploma to me, Mr. Fadlallah laughed and hugged me. He knew the following day was my mom's birthday and how important it was for her to see me graduate. He later revealed to me how important it was for *him* to see me graduate, and that he was so proud of me. Imad Fadlallah left a mark on me. He taught me to see the good in people, to be the best version of myself, and that justice was worth fighting for. When he passed away, I felt as if I had lost my father for the second time."

It was a common sentiment, for Baba built a reputation for showing up to fatherless or troubled homes and pulling students from their state of slumber into a pursuit of success. His bold love left students no choice but to reflect as Asia, Alicia, Adnan, and Mohammad had: *what does he see in me that I fail to see in myself?* This question inspired Fordson's revolution, from mayhem in the Class of '05 to monumental feats for the Class of '09—the most accomplished class in FHS history across countless metrics, including Ivy League and college acceptances. Until the Class of '10 outdid them. This was all despite Baba inheriting a Fordson High that had sent just one student from the Class of '04 to U of M – Ann Arbor—and zero to the Ivy Leagues. In an article for the Arab American News, Julia Kassem—daughter of Dr. Kassem—helped capture the scale of this revolution:

> "By 2010, more than 120 of Fadlallah's students had been accepted at the University of Michigan – [Ann Arbor]. Nearly 80 attended and many went off to attend Ivy League universities. Many attended under the Brehm Scholarship, which many students said motivated them to attend larger and more prestigious universities."[57]

And in 2011, while nearing the end of his road at Fordson, Baba was also on tour with Rashid Ghazi and the other cast members of the acclaimed documentary, *Fordson: Faith, Fasting, Football.* They visited the likes of Stanford University, Oxford University in London, and countless film festivals where they won one award after another and eventually se-

---

57 "Dearborn educator's sudden death shocks community." *Arab American News.* Published March 17, 2017, by Julia Kassem.

cured AMC's only independent film distribution deal awarded that year.[58]

During this time, when I desperately needed to write to my father and hear his voice jump off the page in return, I too would be buried in work—teaching, assistant coaching varsity basketball, and driving three hours roundtrip to earn my master's in education, all while racing towards my destruction in unprecedented fashion: putting on 50-plus pounds while continuing to feast on egg-and-cheese croissants at Burger King, experiencing never before seen symptoms such as darkening teeth and warts on my wrist, and continuing to "cope" on the weekends.

When my two-year commitment with the Teach for America Corps ended, I called Baba: "Baba, I want to move home, but I can't live *at* home. Can I move into the condo?"

I was referring to the one he and Mama owned in Ann Arbor that they had been offering rent-free to lower-income students who attended U of M. He tried to convince me to come home to Dearborn, but that option was an impossibility in my mind since I hoped to live a "free" life.

So, he and Mama lent me over $30,000 to remodel the condo's basement and build my recording studio. I used the money left to buy microphones and other recording technology as I taught myself to produce, engineer, and record. I was officially an "artist"—recording and releasing music under the moniker of PersonALIty as I lived out the delusion of

---

58   March Forth: *From The Prison of Minds* is the book that Principal Fadlallah promised at the end of the "Fordson movie."

"my dream."

Meanwhile, on Twitter, I would rediscover Imam Ali (as) by way of an account dedicated to tweeting *hadith* from him and the other Infallibles of Islam. My curiosity about these tweets would reignite the letters between me and Baba in 2012, just as I was reaching the climax of self-destruction, and about to enter a one-week manic episode characterized by insomnia, severe delusions, and alarming signs of bipolar disorder. While the manic episode itself would last one week, some delusional symptoms would last years—a sentence in the darkness of solitary confinement.

> Ali <email redacted>
> Sat, Apr 28, 2012, 6:34 AM
> to Imad
> Hi Baba,
> This quote from Imam Hassan Al-Askari speaks to how I'm starting to feel in life, now. In fact, for a while now, but now much more deeply:
> "A man who finds intimacy with Allah feels lonely among people."

> Imad <email redacted>
> Mon, Apr 30, 2012, 5:41 AM
> to Ali
> Imam Ali (as) also said:
> "Every breath you take is a step towards death." [and]:
> "The world is like a serpent, so soft to touch, but so full of lethal poison. Unwise people are allured by it and

drawn towards it, and wise men avoid it and keep away from its poisonous effects."

He also said to the world, "I have divorced you three times upon which you may not return to me. Fool someone else, fool someone else, fool someone else." (In Islam when a man divorces the same woman three times it is *haram*[59] to remarry her).

Sent from my iPad

Ali <email redacted>
Mon, Apr 30, 2012, 5:45AM
to Imad

When you say, "He says to the world," you mean he says this to the evil world? Like he's addressing the devil, telling him, "Fool someone else, fool someone else, fool someone else?" Is that correct?

Imad <email redacted>
Mon, Apr 30, 2012, 6:00AM
to Ali

He is referring to the attractions and pleasures of life. Especially things that are forbidden but that people do for satisfaction. Sleeping with a very pretty married woman may give a great pleasure but the cost is hell in the afterlife. The same with alcohol and drugs.

Sent from my iPad

Ali <email redacted>

---

59   Religiously forbidden (thus a cause for sin).

Mon, Apr 30, 2012, 6:19 AM

to Imad

It depends on the drug. I do not believe the cannabis plant (marijuana) is haram. There is too much evidence to suggest otherwise.

I want to sit with you and another wise Muslim theologian; one that is humble, open-minded, intellectual, and willing to consider.

I don't like bringing this up because I know it bothers you, but part of our duty as Muslims is to question and search. Not just accept... how can I accept that a plant is wrong when it directs one's thoughts to feel closer to Allah?

Less than 20 minutes later, as I sat impatiently awaiting his reply, I persisted:

Ali <email redacted>

Mon, Apr 30, 2012, 6:36 AM

to Imad

Bob Marley was one of the most religious, spiritual, revolutionary men to ever live. I forgot what the number was, but one time you told me that Allah had designated a certain number of prophetic figures to come after Muhammad. Not prophets, of course, but prophetic icons. Somewhere in the thousands. I forgot what it was. But anyway, I guarantee you that Bob Marley was one of them. He spread love all over the world through his music and speeches and interviews and fought oppression all over the world. He once said, "Of course the White man grows up hateful. Their parents teach them that the cannabis plant is bad. Forbidden."

He believed it was God's gift of healing. Millions of people across the globe believe the same. Lebanese do not believe so because we associate hasheesh with the gangsters. Americans don't believe so because the country teaches us that it is bad and harmful. But there is a whole rest of the world out there that does not agree!

As for Bob Marley, I believe he indulged too much. He did not practice moderation. But I also believe it was necessary to show the world its positive effects. It only makes people more loving and peaceful; he was one of the most loving and peaceful and productive men to ever live.

Baba went silent. He was likely too busy healing from the heartbreak this email gave him, while taking heed to the strategy of Imam Ali (as), which he had studied and mastered: "Verily, silence is often the most eloquent reply."

It was some weeks after this exchange when the manic episode ensued—induced by the very drug I was defending. If I learned anything that week, as I sat alone on a bench in the Ann Arbor woods during the wee hours, with my nails sinking into my head, it was that the mind can be an utterly horrifying place; and mine had become the worst kind of prison imaginable. For seven days, I slept minimal hours, tweeting around the clock until an old friend caught on and reached out to make sure I was okay. He was unconvinced by my response and called Izzy, who, six years prior, and after his own string of panic attacks, urged me to join him in quitting: "It's a lot more powerful than we think, bro. It happens to a lot of us. We just don't talk about it."

Izzy tried again to reason with me before calling Baba, who showed up at the condo like he was ready for combat—for he would have to pry off the *shaytaan* who rode on my back, dictating my misguided steps. But before showing up that day—when he forced me to pack a duffle bag and get in the car with him to move home to Dearborn—Baba also made a few last attempts to reason:

Imad <email redacted>
Thu, Jun 14, 2012, 12:59 AM
to Ali

I cannot believe this is really happening. I cannot comprehend how you have slipped away under my eyes. All along I befriended you and treated you as an equal with the utmost love and respect... Now I see you fading away before my eyes, and I cannot even throw you a life jacket. In the best possible scenario and assuming everything you are telling me is true; I am not satisfied. On the other hand, if [only] some of what you are saying is not true, the matter is worse.

Your mother, your sisters, your brother and his wife, and I are confused and distraught with what you are doing. I have known you all your life to be loving, caring, and extremely sensitive to the feelings of people around you. Most of all, you were never selfish.

I am not satisfied with your explanation; I am not convinced that you are being reasonable with your decision-making process. You keep telling me to trust you. I do not know the new you. I do not know who this new 'PersonAlity' is.

I want my son back. I want the man I saw in Clarksdale full of life and ambition and attainable goals. I do not want fame on the account of dignity and honor. The behavior you are exhibiting is very scary to say the least. It is your duty and responsibility toward God to allay our feelings and sooth our pain before anything else. Yes, before the fame you want to attain, the world you want to change, and everything else you dream of doing.

It is not too late for you to reconsider your moves. It is not too late for you to come home and take a break from the path you are following. It is not too late for you to reevaluate your path.

Everyone is unhappy with what is going on. I do not think you are happy either. Listen to the people who love you and care unconditionally about you. Listen to the voice of reason.

Ali <email redacted>
Thu, Jun 14, 2012, 4:18 AM
to Imad
If I am wrong, I will come home Sunday, and go to Lebanon with you.
Love you.

Ali

Imad <email redacted>
Sat, Jun 16, 2012, 3:37 PM
to Ali

If you were feeling what I am feeling you will write a
song that will put you on top of the world. If your heart
is aching the way my heart is bleeding, you will paint
pictures with your words.

If your emotions are flowing the way mine are you will
move mountains.

But you are a son and not a father. I want to hug you
kiss you sniff you smell you cuddle you and tell you
how much I love you. How much we all love you. I beg
you to trust me and God is my witness, I will not lead
you astray.

It was Baba's bold love, and my own spiritual journey during
this depressive time, that sparked my inner revolution. There
was the night I sat cross-legged and pleaded to Allah (swt):

"Allah, I know I don't deserve a prophet or angel to show
up, but if you can just give me some sign to know You're there
and listening, I would be very grateful."

Nights later, I questioned God on how I can trust the
Quran when it could have been manipulated, only to open it
and land on 15:9 where my answer awaited: "We have, without

doubt, revealed the Reminder, and We will, without doubt, preserve it."

Then there was the time I pleaded with Allah (swt) about weed, asking whether it was *haram*, and praying that the answer would encourage my habit. Instead, the answer came in the form of an anxiety attack the next time I smoked. When I ignored this sign, and indulged again, the manic episode ensued. Until finally, there was the ceremonious night when I walked to a dumpster and tossed out my large stash, vowing to never touch it again.

> All this paranoia would just make my head enormous
> But alone I felt great, blaze a forest, make a chorus
> I blazed to get deep; to free stress; to feel the best
> I blazed the best; I blazed the meds
> I blazed more than Marley's dreads
> And I know many men, many friends, simply dread
> Lettin' go of weed to cope instead of bein' braindead
> 'Cause we numb; numb til' dumb
> Dumb to think we heal with meds
> 'Cause we don't, nope, spend instead:
> More time in bed; more money for the best
> More in debt as eyes bled, more regret
> More time wasted not facin' it instead, khayeh
> I truly lost my mind some recent times I blazed
> And if you even sorta know me
> You know I used to sing its praise
> So I'm just warnin' you, like a few had warned me
> Wish I listened; was imprisoned; zombie:

Awake, but sleep
I think I had to see my parents weep to regain sight
Ironic: was a "high-on," but rarely high on… *life*
-*Blueberry Mary, 2013*

Weeks after coming home, I boarded a plane with Baba to Libnan, spending most of my hours hyper-analyzing lyrics to songs that I believed were cryptic messages revealing imminent dangers in the world. I had reached rock bottom and was being monitored by Baba around the clock. With my new free time, I began reading *The Autobiography of Malcolm X*. I was gripped from the beginning, studying each page carefully as I tried to locate myself in Malcolm's transformation from pimp to Hajj; from inmate to intellect; from Detroit boy to international ambassador for Islam; from Malcolm Little to Malcolm X to Hajj Malik El-Shabazz.

As I reached the last chapter, I found myself in tears for a third time, for I was enamored by Malcolm and heartbroken by his assassination. I was eager to share his story with Baba. I began recounting passages from the book to him, and he would nod, acknowledging my commentary, but seemingly unsatisfied with it. I was hurt and disappointed; *was he distracted, or did he not think this was important?*

"What's the problem?" I asked.

"What?"

"Here I am getting closer to Islam, and I'm trying to share stories with you from a great Muslim, and you're not interested. You don't like Malcolm X?"

"That's not true."

"Then what?" I asked.

"Nothing."

"Well, I don't get it. I'm sharing this with you because I want to be like him; isn't that a good thing?"

"Like Malcolm X?" He asked.

"*Yeah!*" I replied, righteously.

"Okay. Well, I want to be like Prophet Muhammad."

I never thought the name of our Prophet (s) could be a punch in my mouth, but on that day it was. I walked away, hoping to find some ice for my bruised ego—an ego that had no choice but to accept defeat and reflect.

I felt in that moment like I imagine some Fordson teachers felt in Baba's presence when he was too concerned about the immediate life outcomes of kids to always "meet teachers where they were at" and start the multi-year journey of bringing them to where they needed to be. In time, I realized he knew all too well that "each breath you take is a step towards death," as he shared from Imam Ali (as); and that life is short and mine was on the line.

Baba knew I—like most Fordson boys and girls—may have desperately needed Malcolm X to splash some water on my face, but if I wanted to survive the desert journey, I needed to drink from the well of Rasul Allah (s). After all, Malcolm became Hajj Malik by following Muhammad (s); and Baba knew that following anyone or anything short of the example set by the Prophet (s) and his Holy Progeny (as) would be a dangerous distraction, a delusional detour from the divine, straight path—*Sirat Al-Mustaqeem*.

Days later, I would travel with my uncle Abdallah to Ethiopia, where I searched for answers in Dire Dawa, located in the Somali Region, the nation's most desolate corner. It was there that I met Ali—a brother who was a couple years younger than me and whose words were as timely as they were wise: "Ali, you know, Americans, dey always say 'time is money,' 'time is money.' But time not money, time is *life*."

Time *is* life, I thought. It felt like mine was expiring.

Eventually, I would return to Ann Arbor and begin working with Chin—my GMAT tutor—as I climbed a steep learning curve to master basic algebra and geometry that I had barely grasped at Fordson High (to be fair, Silver and Riley were good math teachers, but the instruction went south after tenth grade). Even six months filled with eight-hour study shifts at U of M's libraries didn't seem to be enough, as I was rejected from three out of the four schools I applied to—and waitlisted at one. But eventually, Baba's *dua*[60] would be answered, and I'd get pulled off the waitlist at Emory University—just in the

---

60   Supplication to God.

nick of time.

And among Baba's many virtues were this: even when it felt like he might leave you in the dust and speed along to his destination, bulldozing over any nonsense along the path, if you kept the door open, you would know he still loved you. And he would even send you a postcard from the promised land—treating you as if you already embodied its roots, upheld its values, and followed in the footsteps of the righteous who traversed it, despite your long way to go.

> Imad <email redacted>
> Thu, May 9, 2013, 5:14 PM
> to Ali
> Dear Son
> I waited until I am in Qulaile to write you. Here I feel I am closer to my father, closer to God, and closer to you. As you start a new journey in your life, I feel obliged to remind you of a few essentials while knowing deep in my heart that with God's help, you have turned the difficult pages of your life and, with His help, have started a new chapter on the road of serving humanity.
> For a while I have been asking God during my prayers to open a path for you and light the way. Your mom called me three times that afternoon while I was praying and, finally, I answered between prayers. She said check your email... I did, and I got down on my knees and thanked Him for His generosity. I had begged of Him to open a path for you, hoping he will do it in September; He opened a highway in May.

As you commence this new challenge, I beg you to remain faithful and thankful for His generosity and His blessings. I beg you to appreciate what He has given you. Something not too many people have. I know my father had it, I know I inherited it from him, and I know you already have it. This gift from God of having a content heart and soul far exceeds everything else any human being can ever attain.

God gives us the tools and the gifts while the instructions are in the heart of the believer. You have the manual in your heart, and with it comes the huge responsibility to make life better for mankind. This is God's expectation after granting His special servants with such a gift.

You have inherited many things from me and from my father. He always told me that he wanted me to be better than him, and he did not mean financially or socially. He wanted me to have better manners so he can be proud. I will echo his words and ask you to be better than both of us. I ask you to keep God and His messenger as your guiding light in life and to thank God 17 minutes a day.

As difficult as the past couple of years were on you, coupled with the near fatal mistakes you have made, I am asking you not to ever entertain such a temporary solution for as long as you live. I know you promised, and you swore on what is dear to you and me and I believe you. Still, I have to remind you. God said:

فَذَكِّرْ إِن نَّفَعَتِ ٱلذِّكْرَىٰ

"Remind, hoping the reminder will be beneficial."
This expedited program will be challenging and difficult. It will require your full attention and will occupy
your days and nights. I know you will rise above the
challenge, just like what you accomplished with the
GMAT. Have an open mind, and entertain and explore
new ideas for the future.
Finally, I want you to know that I enjoyed very much
having you at home the past few months. You know I am
always a phone call away and when you are in doubt,
do not hesitate to ask. Despite everything, you must
know that I am very proud of you and will always be.
With love
Baba

One year and a half later, when I prepared to graduate from
Emory, and was working hard to calculate my next move, I
sent an email to my parents asking them not to press me about
next steps, as I had my heart set on the Doctor of Education
Leadership Program at Harvard and did not want to be cau-
tioned about not having enough "Plan Bs."

Imad <email redacted>
Mon, Sep 23, 2013, 11:57 PM
to Ali
Jig I will not ask you and I am not worried about you. I
know you are on God's side and He will guide you every

step of the way.

الله يوفقك

Not long after, I was encouraging Baba to apply as well so he could join me.

> Ali <email redacted>
> Mon, Dec 2, 2013, 11:44 AM
> to Imad
> You should apply Jig. You have almost 2 weeks. You can start your own educational consulting company. You do not need to return to the district.

> Ali <email redacted>
> Mon, Dec 2, 2013, 11:46 AM
> to Imad
> Actually Jig, you should apply next year. You will need to study for and take the GRE. :-)

That was where our letters ended. But a little more than three years later, after Baba had passed away, and I was finally experiencing the light of healing on the other side, I stumbled upon a letter from Imam Ali (as) to his holy sons and successors, Imam Hassan and Imam Husayn (as). Tears welled in my eyes, trickling slowly down my cheeks, as I felt the presence of my father, for he had dedicated so much of his time and study to model his speech after the Holy Prophet (s) and his Progeny (as):

> "My dear son! You are part of my body and soul and whenever I look at you, I feel as if I am looking at myself. If any calamities befall you, I feel as if they have befallen me. Your death will make me feel as if it was my own death. Your affairs are, to me, like my own affairs.
>
> Therefore, I committed these pieces of advice to paper. I want you to take care of them, to pay attention to them, and to guard them well. I may remain longer in your life, or I may not, but I want these pieces of advice to remain with you always.
>
> My first and foremost advice to you, my son, is to fear Allah. Be His obedient servant. Keep His thought always fresh in your mind. Be attached to and carefully guard the principles (Islam), which connect you with Him. Can any other connection be stronger, more durable, and more lasting than this?"

This short excerpt from the letter felt as if Baba was putting into perspective why he kept writing to me while I was locked up in the prison of my mind; for in time, as I absorbed his words, and pieced together his letters, they molded into a golden key that unlocked the prison door within and ushered me into freedom. Though not before I mourned and grieved—not only my past, but also, and more-so, the backbreaking reality of a future without my father.

Next page; met bestie in seventh grade
Things got messy in eleventh grade
So we fell out; I appeared in his dream
He appeared at my job
We repaired n' redeemed
Then we were good again; five years
Then I really started facing my fears
Is God real? What would it mean?
What would I change? Man, it would seem
To really take the fun out of my life
Parties, women, 'the high life'
But I gave it up, for the self-love
N' as I made changes I felt judged
So 'we grew apart,' as the story goes
But we're just two sides of an Oreo
'Cause that middle White bigot did us damage
And we just tryna' manage a victory-o
Though I wonder, did you feel judged, too?
Given that I really used to nudge you?
Like, 'Bro please, smoke less weed;
I tell you what you need, 'cause I love you.'
Just the other day we reconnected
Such a great spirit, don't neglect it
Am I a broken record? I hope you nod
I was duped into doubt, til' I gave it to God
At the end of 24, you're my brother
Don't have many more with each other
I'm not really sure how you ration it all

But all along bro, compassion is all
I have ever felt as far as you're concerned
Learned to not concern myself with your concerns
I know, you never asked me to play that role
But you know I always dove to save that ball
And the thing is, you are that same dude
If you gave *you* love you gave to
Your exes, or better yet, your Exits
You'd pass the real test, 'cause you'd save you

-Return to Love, 2019

PART III

HOMECOMING

"The death of a father breaks one's back."

-Imam Ali ibn Abi Taleb (as)

12. (STILL) BROKEN

The Worst Day of My Life

It was before *fajr*[61] on Monday, March 13th, 2017. Baba awoke wearing his V-neck white tee tucked into the brand-new pajama pants Mama had just bought him, which he wore above his bellybutton. He swung his long legs to the right until his bare feet grasped the cold surface of the bedroom's hardwood floors, tapping his feet briefly until they found the open slots of his Moroccan blue, worn-out slippers. And he rose, taking three steps forward before turning in front of the footboard to Mama—locking eyes with his soulmate one last time, then falling gracefully toward his sudden death.

Three missed calls from my sister Rima awoke me after midnight in Los Angeles, and when I called back, she answered with a one-sentence story broken between sniffles: "Ali, something happened, and Baba fell, and he died."

My passageway through whatever stages of grief—shock, denial, bargaining, acceptance—lasted altogether about two or three seconds, as if her word "died" was a missile that swept me up and carried me into space to explore each stage, an

---

61   Dawn.

out-of-body experience moving me through planets of grief, each with unique temperatures and emotions, until this fateful missile circled back into my chest, ending me, killing the version of myself I was before he left.

My best friend was gone.

But the worst day of my life didn't arrive until seventy-three days later, on May 25. I was seated a few rows from the front of the stage where I was preparing to accept my diploma for a doctorate in education leadership from Harvard University, seated under the same stadium-sized tent in Radcliffe Yard where Baba and I sat together just three years prior to watch the famous educator Dr. Geoffrey Canada deliver a riveting keynote speech—a blend of stand-up comedy and serious candor that had me thinking as much about the wisdom behind Baba's laughter as I was about America's (mis) education system. Dr. Canada was only warming up—and warming Baba up to him—when he made the joke about education being "the only business where you don't need patent attorneys, since you gotta beg people to steal your good ideas!"

Baba giggled helplessly, leaving a smile plastered on his face until Canada turned the smile straight just minutes later: "They call some schools dropout factories, but that doesn't really explain the fact that there are *entire communities* where kids haven't received an education, *in decades.*"

My heart sank as Baba exhaled his stress. And then he was smiling again. "If you want people to like you, get outta education," Canada continued. "Go sell stocks and bonds. People like to beat on me the most because I say, 'We should fire lousy teachers.' I didn't say we should hate them, or beat their dogs. I didn't even say the *mediocre* ones. I just said the lousy ones…we should fire them! So my oldest son's a lawyer; he calls me and says, 'Dad, all my friends are mad with you.' I said 'Why?' He said, 'It's all over the internet that you said we should send all the lousy teachers to the middle-class communities.' Well, I *did* say that, but that wasn't the complete quote. What I said was, 'If we can't get rid of them, *then* we should send them to the middle-class communities!' Because they wouldn't tolerate it for a second. It wouldn't be my problem anymore. But there would be a solution!"

Baba was loving it, and I was feeling more accomplished for bringing him that day of joy than I did for bringing myself to Harvard on a full ride. By the time the weekend was done, we were both so fired up, Baba started to wonder whether he should take my advice from that prison letter one year prior and apply to my program, too. "You'd be *perfect*," I pleaded.

But three years later, on that graduation day—as I sat there sporting my doctoral cap and gown, with double-socks on to try to fill the extra half inch on the size thirteen suit shoes that I took from Baba's closet before his belongings were donated by Mama—I neither felt sad for myself for Baba's absence, nor sad for my family, for we all felt his presence.

Yet an old, familiar pain arose inside, slithering up like a venomous snake from the pit of my broken heart, stirring inside like a tornado until it touched down. This sea of sadness erupted into a storm, seemingly unprompted like torrential rain from a blue sky, jolting me forward as I tried to process it, with no drugs to blame it on, for they had now been cleansed from my system for over five years—only sobering tears that raced down my face and traced my lips, making me taste the salty poison of this pain again.

I was broken. *Still* broken.

The evidence spilled in my ferocious weep, now as uncontrollable as it was unanticipated, and so I pressed my face into the calluses of my palms, a hopeless attempt to contain my tears, as my classmates Kerry and Ola—who had just journeyed alongside me through the lush mountains of Libnan, with Baba as our joyous tour guide—welled up, their own tears trickling as they rubbed my back. And as grateful as I was for their love, their rub became like nails on the chalkboard of my body, because my grief was only growing, with no end in sight, and I knew nothing about the source of this sudden anguish.

And yet I knew everything about it. I knew it wasn't Baba's absence that tortured me in that moment, but rather the realization that he fought and died to make this moment possible for me, and you, and others on the margins. I knew that he sacrificed his own dreams so that I would not only see this Harvard stage, but be seen on it, and seen correctly: Arab—not White; Muslim—not threatening; American—not anti. I knew he fought so that I, too, could be seen in a box—yes, a box—like Africans and Asians, because Baba knew I had to first exist in a box before breaking free from its limitations.

Baba knew this long before he was Fordson High's principal, even long before he was Stout Middle School's principal, for he was no stranger to incidents like the one at Stout when

Mrs. Youmans, his school counselor, phoned him in panic: "Imad, I was just talking to this sixth grader! Nothing was wrong! He just dove beneath the desk! He's shaking and crying and won't move!"

Baba sprinted out of his office and down the hall toward the boy, who was new from Yemen. And as he ran, he heard a helicopter flying over Stout, its propellers reverberating through the windows of the school courtyard, where the ten chickens who lived in it squawked as they took cover, and its floor-to-ceiling glass rumbled as he ran past, all as Baba's brain calculated, quickly realizing that the boy must've heard the helicopter himself and associated the noise with the sound of fighter jets in his homeland. So, Baba asked no questions. He just took the boy into his arms, soothing this terrified child whose skin camouflaged into the dark shadows beneath the desk where he took cover from the British colonizer whose Caucasian box he was now told to check.

Baba knew this well before he held this boy because Baba *was* this boy: hiding throughout the 1970s as families were slaughtered by the dozens, terror overcoming him as he feared being found by the sound of his trembling bones; watching refugee camps nearby get bombarded by israeli bomber jets overhead; sprinting to an underground shelter in *Tebnine* with his baby siblings in his arms as they dodged israeli missiles, running until his flat feet were cut and calloused through the holes in his shoes, running until decades later when he could finally catch his breath and reflect in his journal:

"I vividly remember having two pairs of pants and four

tops. One pair of shoes with holes in the soles the size of a quarter. I understood my father's situation and was ashamed to ask him for new soles, so I'd rip the cardboard covers off my notebook and shove them in my shoes so the bottom of my feet would not touch the ground."

He knew these stories should be acknowledged, at least. That they should count for something on a census. That we should be visible in our Yemeni or Lebanese or otherwise Arab skin when we enter hallways. That our low exam scores, broken Englishes, and refugee statuses should somehow be captured in the story of Dearborn Public Schools, where our erasure began the day our data was dismissed by the district who, seemingly overnight, stopped reporting our test scores under a separate "Arab" category, instead forcing us into a so-called Caucasian box, thus disguising our deficient scores, colorful identities, and generational traumas.

And Baba knew it wasn't always this way; he knew that it was a deliberate decision by the district because the gap between Caucasian and Arab students became so wide that the district feared what our parents would do. *Ask*: Why are my kids underperforming? *Ask*: What supports are they not receiving? *Ask*: Why are we treated inferior to Whites? Indeed, to label us Caucasian was to wash away the evidence on the scene of educational crimes; to silence our protest; to hide behind the guise of "colorblindness" that Baba famously made synonymous with "stupid" in an interview with the *Arab American News*. Because Baba knew all too well that they made a mockery of us by calling us "White"—knowing we're precluded from their privileges, yet promised the punishment that White systems of power deliver to people of color.

And so, as I walked across that Harvard stage, having just lost Baba and gained a degree that was a pipedream for the both of us, I realized this feeling of inadequacy that lurked like my shadow had continued to carry its gloom into each new graduation or the like. That this gloom could color any great day invisible, just like my identity. That a Harvard degree could cure nothing of the bitterness I felt. That this bitterness had not only failed to disappear after all these years, but grown. And I despised this bitterness. And I despised myself for it, the way I despised the dark cloud of cigarette smoke that filled the lungs of my father—and at times, my own lungs—and helped accelerate his end.

And on May 25, seventy-three days after Baba died, I despised all of it more than ever before.

Because it was during this milestone of a moment, one I tried my very best to trivialize for a fourth time *(enough with the hoopla; just gimme my degree)*, that the truth surfaced like an earthquake. The truth was, I not only cared to be there, but I cared so much so that I believed diplomas were pieces in the puzzle of becoming whole again. I believed degrees were answers to questions I was terrified to ask: What do I need to heal from? How will I? Can I?

And so, when I tried yet again to reduce this moment to a trivial ritual, I must have realized deep in my subconscious that this "silly ritual" was the symbol of Baba's fight, that this moment was tantamount to a tremendous pursuit, and that he was our fallen army general in the ongoing war for it: the pursuit of being—and of being seen as—whole and human.

And what hurt the most from that moment before I was called onto the stage, when the dam of my bitterness was broken, and violent waves of agony that I could not verbalize crashed the walls of my insides before raining down like hail, was not only the realization that Mr. Fadlallah, The Principled Principal, spent a lifetime fighting for one simple demand—fairness—but also this: that despite Baba fighting the forces of hate with every fraction of his being, I was still unsure how successful he was in securing this basic human right for the four little boys and girls he fathered. That his public-school pride ate him alive when his first three kids were failed by Fordson High, and my mother fought for my baby sister Silan to forgo Fordson's sinking ship for a fairer shot in private school. And, worst of all, that although he revolutionized Fordson and awakened its families, Baba died on the losing side of his effort to deliver a fair education to the doorstep of all children and families in Dearborn.

So, I suppose that graduation day was the ultimate symbol of my sadness—and of Baba's sadness. I suppose that the sound of my name on that stage was a sobering statement. That reading my degree was like reading a memoir of my mourning, like the morning after March 13th when I awakened into day two of our living nightmare on Neckel St., already dressed in full black before I rolled out of bed and began heading downstairs where a crowd awaited in our family room, and it only took a peripheral glimpse of his already-framed picture before my knees buckled and my legs failed beneath me, my face bursting into anguish as I collapsed on our stairs midway down.

I suppose that graduation ceremony saddened me because of the contents within those chapters of an unpublished book—*The Prison of Minds*—that Baba had left behind. I was sad not because it remained unpublished, but because despite its historical accounts, his book, I knew, was not about history. For the history he shared, each detail of each day, was handpicked from 1,000 acres of history to help showcase our present day.

And so, despite the countless reasons to be grateful for that graduation stage, I was forced to face a reality that overshadowed them all: I am sad. Sad for our children and families. Sad despite their triumphs in the face of treachery. Sad despite the dozens of elite college admits from Fordson and Dearborn High and Edsel Ford who now decorate the @Dearborn Instagram page each year. Sad despite the rise of Fordson alumni into the annals of history: from the first Arab and Muslim NFL head coach to our first Arab and Muslim mayor of Dearborn.

I am stricken with this sadness of no cure except a revolution in Dearborn Public Schools. A sadness that emerged from where my bitterness was submerged before it overtook me all at once.

And this sadness that consumed me, was also due to a great contradiction, one that tormented me for a decade. It's a contradiction I was once ashamed of and should confess, in part because I suspect you feel the same, and it is this: all those years I couldn't, and still today cannot, help but feel that Dearborn Public Schools was undeserving of my father's gifts, and unworthy of his intoxicating love and his irresistible presence and his spell-binding smile.

I couldn't help but feel like the wisdom of a man who memorized tapes imbued with hundreds of spiritual truths from our Holy Prophets (s) and Imams (as) was somewhat wasted. That a man equipped to help nations make big demands was reduced to roaming a bigot-filled building in a suburb, to demand the basics: to exist, to be seen, to be safe, to be heard, to be fairly served by our miseducation system.

And yet, because of the absence of fairness at Fordson High, and because of the deliberate design behind this reality: the silent agreement among bigots to place invisible bars between us and our dreams, and flip off the switch of our minds, and welcome us with crossed arms into a gorgeous complex of a school where our futures are on the line, and where we offer our bodies wholly, with a grimace for gameday and a smile for Saturday; because of this place Baba coined *The Prison of Minds*; and, most importantly, because of the beautiful children, the innocent prisoners, including the invisible Arabs like you and me, who were nurtured with hate in our most-vulnerable state, and who loved, often even our wardens, despite it—because of this all, I know, and have always known, that the war Baba waged against Dearborn's hate is the most worthwhile war, and that our families were most worthy of a warrior like him, and that our students were most deserving of his intoxicating love and his irresistible presence and his spell-binding smile.

"When the time came for my father to pass away, he hugged me and said, 'O, my dear son! I advise you to do what my father advised me to do at the time of his death, and what his father had advised, likewise. My son! Be patient with the truth, even if it be bitter.'"

-Imam Muhammad ibn Ali ibn Husayn (as)

13. GRIEVING

Baba's death was the closest I ever felt to Allah (swt). It felt like Allah ordered one of His angels to lower his lofty wing and place me in it—in the haven of utmost protection, covered in God's mercy. For moments I would feel unfathomable pain… and then Allah (swt) would shield me from it, as if allowing me to glimpse the state of helplessness I would be in if not for His comfort. The feeling was palpable—so much so that for those first days or weeks, my prayer rug became the only place I could cry, as if its surface was the angel's wing. When I would approach my *msalliyeh*,[62] I would feel the force of it like a black hole, seizing me quicker than quicksand, sucking me into the abyss of my emotional despair. Yet I would also feel relief as I fell to my knees, the *msalliyeh* offering me my only protection from the grim world beyond it. And so, I found my deepest gratitude to God not in the joys of laughter and light, but in the utter helplessness of grieving.

Some days, I felt isolated and lonely in a crowd of mourners; while other days, I found solace in community. We knew Dearborn would mourn, yet still, the outpouring of love was overwhelming. And as we arrived in Qulaile to bury Baba,

---

62   Prayer rug/mat.

his secrets were exposed before us. Enormous banners began appearing on the main road before Qulaile and covered all corners of the village. They were decorated with Baba's image and Arabic phrases such as, "Gone is the father of the orphans and the poor" and "A star of Allah was lost." Most villagers swarmed the streets, weeping, while others stood in salute from their balconies. When it was time to bury him, the villagers and guests surrounded Baba in silence, honoring his spirit, and allowing his body to enter the ground peacefully. His burial was nothing short of blessed. It was beautiful.

Afterward, we gathered at our Qulaile home, where villagers arrived by the dozens. They recalled the stories of people like Daoud, a young man in his twenties who went on a burglary spree around the village, eventually landing at our home where he stole all the valuables he could find—including a six-millimeter gun that belonged to my deceased *jido*,[63] a former police officer in the *jnoub*. The stolen six-millimeter—more than anything—upset Baba, who cherished the keepsake, and who was in Michigan during the robbery, yet no less determined to catch the thief. Baba downloaded the footage from his hidden cameras and brought it to the Wayne County Sheriff's Office to enhance an image of Daoud, before providing it to Mr. Ramadan, the head prosecutor in the jnoub. The young man was promptly arrested and imprisoned; but not before Baba made him confess to whom he sold the gun. Weeks later, upon arriving in Libnan, Baba tracked down the gun's new owner and purchased it back at the man's asking

---

63 Grandpa.

price. Oum Daoud,[64] upon knowing that Baba was in town, arrived at his doorstep pleading with him to somehow get her son out of jail.

That day, Prosecutor Ramadan phoned my mother's father, Lebanon's President of Parliament: "*Raees*,[65] with all due respect, is your son-in-law in his right mind? He's insisting I release the prisoner who robbed his home!"

I can imagine the smile on my *jido's* face as he responded, "Fulfill his wish."

It was reminiscent of the many times I stood by my father in my *jido's* home, as Baba asked the *raees* for one *wasta*[66] after another, until one day Jido turned to me and said, "I wish that *just once*, your father would request something for himself!"

When Daoud was released, Baba took him under his wing, counseling him, and convincing him to visit the villagers he robbed and apologize to each of them. Meanwhile, Baba gave Oum Daoud the money she needed to recompense these families for their stolen items and damages.

Arriving back in Dearborn, we entered our home, and Mama erupted into tears, devastated. We assumed it was all the things one might assume—being in the house without Baba, losing the love of her life, being hit yet again with the trembling realization of his absence. But what prompted this outburst was still unbeknownst to us, for Mama had peered out of the window to notice that somehow, the apple tree Baba

---

64 Mother. In this case: mother of Daoud.

65 President.

66 Favor (by way of a personal connection).

planted two decades prior, which began bearing fruit years before his passing, had been chopped down. While we were in Libnan burying Baba, the city had shown up and cut down the medium-sized tree without Mama consenting or being consulted, supposedly out of fear that one day it may interfere with the electrical wires erected a couple dozen feet above it.

It was bizarre. To me, it represented the end of the fruits Baba could bear. The man who once gifted me the book *The Giving Tree* by Shel Silverstein was now like the tree personified in the story: a stump or a tombstone to rest upon. I could visit him for inspiration, but the fruits of his wisdom I once took for granted were no longer low-hanging, no longer dangling before my distracted eyes. Now, I would have to retrace my roots to find fruit in the tree of our lineage. And to pay it forward like he had, I would have to reform my lot to prepare new soil and plant my own trees. Meanwhile, Dr. Jewell-Sherman mailed a new apple tree to our home, hoping the new roots would at least serve as a reminder of Baba's spirit.

Days after that dreadful Harvard graduation, I booked an Airbnb in Salem, Massachusetts for myself and Mama, hoping it might offer us a small escape, a short sabbatical after a weekend of festivities. We settled in, walked the town, and got ready for bed early. I couldn't recall sleeping next to Mama before that night in Salem, at least not since childhood.

After she fell asleep, she kept sleep-talking to me as if I was Baba, mumbling "Imad," followed by a complaint or a command: "Imad, turn the light down, please." "Imad, stop making noise, please."

And on she went, for an hour, as tears raced down my face. The idea that her subconscious had not yet accepted his loss tormented me. The idea that she was still married in her sleep state. Still married in the subconscious of her mind. Still sleeping next to her soulmate.

It was months after Baba passed when I left my L.A. apartment and retreated into the backwoods of Chattahoochee Hills, a rural town nearby Atlanta International Airport, where I planned to help finish Baba's book. But all I could seem to do for a week was cry, and the only ink that would pour from my pen was poetry. It was as if Allah (swt) was letting me know: *you* brought yourself here to *write*…but I brought you here to *mourn*.

And so, I surrendered my week to that task, letting the ink of trauma and tears of grief spill simultaneously, as I spoke to the spirit of Baba that I prayed still loomed.

Baba

your Imam Ali go-to hadith was a death tease:

ask me, before you lose me

fear would stick its sharp fingers

through my throat and grip my gut

when it fell on my ears

You'd always say

the spirit of language is lost in translation

but how could you say that

When your translation

left me certain

I would lose my *Imad;* my foundation?

Baba
you left
and with you
left my fixation on making you proud
replaced with recognition
that this too, in fact
was what Rasul Allah called
minor polytheism
tell me, Baba
how did i manage
to make you the idol
you begged me to never believe in?
admitting you had to go
for me to truly go to God
feels like saying
i helped kill you

Ya Sayyed
the baby spider stands on the spine
of my journal
and though i'm scared
i massage my words around it
because when i, as your young son
murdered one
and you stood witness
you sat me down to share the story
of the miracle in the cave
God used the spider to shield Rasul Allah
they formed webs in his cave to confuse the transgressors
who turned away
so, i thought
what if this spider who stands on the spine
of my journal
descends from the spider
who saved the Messenger
we descended from?
in an age where we kill spiders
like we tie shoelaces
you taught me to honor them
which i know you'd agree deserves no applause
for what fool must i be to kill a fellow creature
let alone one who may save me?

Baba
once upon that time
before you had two tongues
but just one
and you sent it searching
in your thick *jnoubeh* accent
for tax support on campus
And they said "Sawsan gets it done"
and you met my beautiful mama
there's no way her good math
accounted for this
your returns came with a wife for life
her service came with the price of a widow
she likes to be seen as one
as much as you like to be seen as "smoker"
but i can't help but wonder
though the answer is obvious
if mama saw how wealthy she'd become
by doing your taxes
and collecting your payments of love
yet how broke she'd become
when your payments stopped so suddenly
would she still have wanted to service you?

Baba
in your silence were the secrets
you didn't care to keep
hidden treasures
buried in the deep south
of your soul
shared only on occasion
yet as often as we took your cues
and used our clues
to ask the right questions
i felt like
i had just found my rhythm, Baba
the right-question-rhythm
the shot-to-your-heart rhythm
when the rhythm of your heart
stopped

Baba
Teta always said about you
if his eyes can see it, his hands can fix it
so is it
that your hand held those cigarettes
like construction workers
awaiting instructions from your eye's crane
as it studied the site of your pain for solutions?
flashes of your father's face
flashes of refugee families in crowded camps
and soldiers sleeping in snow-covered caves
as they defend the land you left?
flashes of the fallen and forgotten
who you never dared forget
flashes you cannot fix
flashes you cannot fix
flashes you cannot fix
not without a flame for your sticks of nicotine
flashes of the ashes
falling on the deaf ears of the oppressor
as their hair stylist
dusts them off with a gold-plated brush
flashes you cannot fix
unless you inhale sticks
which you knew
which you knew
would re-erect themselves
one by one

around your arteries around your heart
stacks of sticks forming bricks of tar
forming a wall
builder of builders
artist of artists
master of hands
and the only thing you ever set your eyes on
which you could not fix
were the flashes
or could you with hands of magic?
quick trigger thumb
flamed between two fingers
90-degree motions
stick after stick after stick
a daily labor of decades
until it was built
until you fixed the only thing you never could and
left us
with flashes

Baba
i never had much in common with
a cold and hungry newborn crying kitten
until your death shrunk me so small
and I curled into a little ball
and Allah gave me refuge in my *msalliyeh*
Like my rug was a warm cloud in the sky
That wrapped my bare bones
with warmth
and provided extra air for my lungs
so i could hold the long monotone
note of my weep
a while longer

Teta
has never talked to me like a friend, Baba
only a beloved grandson
we know her love is the fountain of forever
she can't even pour me tea
without pouring poetry into me
poured and poured
reetak tu'burneh, ya ghali intah
and poured and poured
ya 3ayoun Teta intah, ya a7la Ali
and poured and poured
until my heart was pregnant
until my stomach protruded
until poetry perspired from my pores
except once
just once
weeks after your death, Baba
she peered deep into my eyes
with her Teta hijab removed
and i stood face to face with Fatimah
just once
her face serious and stern
just once prioritizing her pain
over my gain:
"i never loved myself" she said to me
sharp pangs of sadness shocked me out of my spoiled
skin
always drunk off her love

into sobriety
just once
for the first time in twenty nine years
in the days before tears would fall
onto the pillows of her death bed
i met the woman who taught me that it was possible
for one to speak no language other than love
yet not even love herself

Baba
your baby brother Hassane
turns from your picture to tell me
i just love his face
and I'm utterly amazed
by the fury of pain
and five sermons
that emerge from five words
and yet there are levels
for when your then only grandson
Zayn
mistakes Hassane's face for yours
and sprints his toddler *teezo*
into his lap yelling
"jido!"
and i watch his senses work in silence
past the clues of new scents
past the confusion
of your continued absence
and draw away from the wrong lap
and draw the right conclusion
only God knows how i—
with my low tolerance for pain—
could've walked on knives
through a pit of fire
as tarantulas feasted on my face
and that would've been laughable
compared to the pain i felt

that moment

and days later when it happened again

Dear Allah,
i pray
that if we make it to *jannah*
you make me a baby
but with my adult brain
just for a day
so baba can carry me around like Zayn
and we can forever remember that day

Baba

it's not that you set the bar so high it was out of reach

it's just that you set the bar so high

i had a lot to learn first

and you a lot to teach

and heavens

it was high

so it left me starving

for your approval

the whole hike up

only to lose you before i gained it

only to realize too late

that i had gained it long ago

is grief gendered?
because men in our family
mourn
exactly like women in our family
(weep generously; wail never)
Al-Fatiha.

"Successful indeed is the one who purifies their soul, and doomed is the one who corrupts it."

-The Holy Quran, 91:9-10

14. HEALING

I never understood the idea of "love at first sight." At best, it felt elusive—more fantasy than fate. Mostly, it felt fake. Until it happened.

At least I thought it did.

I remember the feeling. The lust that ruled the last five years of my adolescent life suddenly lost grip of the wheel as a deeper something stepped into the driver's seat of my heart, shifting the gears of my feelings, moving me toward an intimacy beyond body and form, my spirit wanting to lunge from my skeleton to find home someplace new. It felt like the sobering silence of time standing still as I stood there. Staring.

It happened a handful of times in my youth, like when I laid eyes on a classmate standing forty feet away in Fordson's hall freshman year. Lust felt like desire, like hunger. But love—at least the only love I knew of—felt like water after a long Ramadan day. Love felt like healing.

Long before I learned that love *is* healing, I would learn that heartbreak liked to disguise itself as love, setting its traps, awaiting the naive and inexperienced to pass by and be seized.

She was hurt long before she hurt me. But I was only under her spell until Amto Rima saw me sitting sad again, this time on Teta's porch, where she made me spill it:

"Did you tell her you love her?

"Excuse me!" she said, slapping my chin up with two fingers. "Did you?!"

"Yeah."

"Ha! I'm gonna kick your a**! You never tell a girl you love her! Understand me?!"

"Did she say it back?!

"Hello!? Who the hell am I talking to?!"

"No."

"Oh, s***!" she said, laughing in pissed-off disbelief.

And that's when boot camp began. My ex-basketball-coach aunt was now teaching me a new game. She used to say, "Play hard!" Now she said, "Play hard-*to-get*;" she used to say, "Faster, Ali!" Now she said, "Slow it down, Ali, reply tomorrow." She used to say, "Shake and bake." Now she said, "Give-and-take!" She used to say, "Use your screen!" Now she said, "Ignore your screen... stop being a sissy, and use her *friends*... to get her jealous."

It wasn't long before the ball was back in my court. But the girl was as brutal as she was beautiful, and we battled through breakups and messy makeups like crazy couples do. On one tormenting afternoon, when my heart was bending toward break, I resorted to calling the radio station (I didn't dare tell Amto Rima).

"Hi, I'm going through something. Can you please play 'Don't Change' by Musiq Soulchild?" I asked.

"Aww, sweetie, you got it," the jockey responded. "Keep

your ear tuned in; you'll hear it soon. Keep your head up honey, okay?"

Part of me was terrified one of the boys would hear me, especially Young Merce, who loved that station and probably put 300 miles per day on his car as he patrolled Dearborn like five-o. He would've spread the word like fire, and I would've gotten roasted—or "gotten my name," as we liked to say—for that one.

But mostly, I didn't even care. I just wanted to hug the feet of that radio jockey when I heard Musiq Soulchild blaring through my speakers ten minutes later as I lay with my arms and legs sprawled on my bed, praying my parents wouldn't interrupt my four-minute moment, as I tried to process, getting lost in the possibilities of true love, still wondering what it meant as I let myself shed a few (hundred) man-tears and feel my heart break and reattach in a vicious loop.

It would take years—filled with a few more heartbreaks, hard lessons, and mourning sessions in bed—before I began learning what true love meant. But by the time I had an idea—or at least the intention to pursue love in a way that was Islamically aligned—I would have to undo layers of trauma, sparked by my "first love" at Fordson, and set ablaze years later, after college, when I was in a so-called committed relationship and cheated on.

> I been single for good reason
> Had internal work to do (yeah)
> It has lasted many seasons
> And was worth the hurtin' too (yeah)
> -Real Love, 2019

Because even after the cheating incident no longer induced visceral pain or anger or heartache of any kind, and even after I forgave and mostly forgot, I was left distrustful of romantic relationships—quick to link any small act to a large crime. So much so that I confessed to my therapist Brent about it, as his eyes widened in surprise that it was my first mention of the incident, despite several years of therapy.

"What are you feeling, Ali?"

"I mean, I know I'm being self-judgmental, and that these are unhealthy thoughts. But I feel stupid—ashamed that I'm still as impacted by it as I am. Like, I know I would do well in a relationship, you know, for the most part; but I also know, if, like, for example, it was early on in getting to know a girl, and we were in a public setting, and she was talking to another guy, maybe even her cousin or an old childhood friend, but I didn't know who he was or how she saw him exactly, I could get easily triggered. Like, I'll shut down and want to stop trusting her. And my body language would follow. And, you know, I'm fine with upholding the standard of what is appropriate behavior as a Muslim, you know; like, even if it never happened to me, a woman who I am getting to know shouldn't be off to the side, for example, talking to a guy and vice versa; I shouldn't be off talking to a girl without pulling one another into the convo. But still, I'm getting triggered in an unhealthy way; and it's like, what do I gotta do to undo the impact of it on me? And part of me wonders if it's still impacting me because I never truly worked through it."

"Have you ever considered what you would tell yourself?

That younger version of Ali?"

"Good question. I mean, I've had that hunch, too, that maybe, subconsciously, I still feel it was my fault somehow—even though rationally I know that's not true. But I think the younger version of me internalized this idea that I didn't earn her loyalty because I wasn't 'bad boy' enough, and she was attracted to that. Like, maybe if I was more of a wild guy, she wouldn't have done that. It feels ugly to say that aloud, but it feels true. And in some weird way, even though I know it's silly, and I would never want to be perceived that way, that's still how the hurt part of me is internalizing things, maybe? Like, maybe if I give too much, or if I'm too genuine, my trust will get abused? I really don't know."

After our session, I reopened the floodgates of my feelings and let those raw emotions resurface as I walked over to my *msalliyeh* to pray *duhr* and *asr*.[67] When I was done, I left my head on the *sejdeh*[68] and spoke to Allah (swt) for a while. Then, I began repeating over and over, maybe fifty times, "____'s actions had nothing to do with me; ____'s actions had nothing to with me; ____'s actions had nothing to do with me…"

I paused between each one, letting it sink in and become less and less awkward, as I knew I was just trying to rewire my trauma circuits to bring myself to a place of healing. I wanted true love, but I didn't want to bring any unhealed baggage into a relationship and have to unpack it there. I wanted to

---

67 Noon and afternoon prayers, respectively.

68 Small tablet of clay or other soil, representative of pure Earth, and used for head-contact during prostration.

be the most whole version of myself, to be best prepared for the soulmate Allah (swt) promised us throughout the Holy Quran, my favorite *ayah*[69] being 30:21:

> *"And among His signs is that He has created spouses from among yourselves for you to live with in tranquility; and He has placed love and mercy between you. Surely, in that are signs for those of you who reflect."*

It was hard work; though I knew that if a God-centered relationship was my true goal, then it was time to let go of Amto Rima's rulebook, retire the mentality that ruled my past, and deepen my relationship with Allah (swt)—who I knew would guide me to "the one." After that session with Brent, when I began the rewiring process, I found the strength to let go, and let God.

Homecoming

The voice of intuition is like the voice of a guiding angel that Allah (swt) appoints within us. The voice of our *fitra*[70] that we—by our own doing—lose the ability to hear over time but that speaks with clarity when we seek it. Even before I

---

69   Verse (Quranic). Literal translation: "sign."

70   Our innate disposition (that recognizes the oneness and omniscience of God, and by extension, the truth).

embraced Islam, I embraced this voice, for I knew that the only time it failed me was when I ignored it. It called me to Minneapolis, Minnesota when I was afraid to leave home. Though I lost my way for a while, Minneapolis helped awaken the academic and servant within me. It then called me to Mississippi to serve in the Teach for America Corps and earn my master's in education. Then it called me back home from Mississippi in 2012 after my teaching service, despite several job offers that promised more security and clarity. Then it called me to Atlanta for my MBA. Then to Cambridge for my doctorate. Then, with my only residency offer coming from Los Angeles during the last year of my doctoral program, it was time, yet again, to relocate.

After years of little contact with ATM, who had been living in L.A. for some time, I gave him a call.

"What can you tell me about housing?" I asked.

"Where you tryin' to live?" He probed.

"I don't know. That's why I called you. Somewhere nice?"

"When you comin'?"

"Like, next week."

"Man, *SubhanAllah*,[71] your timing is crazy. My contract is expiring here in Koreatown. I want to move to a nicer area, maybe West Hollywood. You tryin' to room?" He asked.

"Woah *woah*, bro, you know I love you, but that's out of the question. I've been living alone for years. I like it that way."

"*Alright*... but if you live alone, the rent is *insane*. Unless you're trying to spend over three stacks per month, it won't

---

71   Praise (be to) God, or Glory to God.

be somewhere nice or near your work." He said.

"You know if we live together there would be *hella* rules, right?" I asked.

"I'm all ears." He said, curiously.

"Like, I'm talkin'... no partying, no women coming in and out, no tomfoolery whatsoever. No college life stuff."

"Not a problem for me," he assured.

"I'm crazy about cleanliness too, bro. Like, dishes-washed-right-after-they're-used type stuff. Clean sink at *all* times."

"Not an issue, bro. You have my word." He added.

"Alright baby boy! Let's do it!"

I was excited—but concerned—about living in L.A. My identity in Islam was growing, and I was well aware of the many anti-Islamic forces that polluted L.A.'s scene. Still, my intuition was confirmed when I visited a beach-front restaurant right after landing at LAX. I stood on the restaurant's balcony overlooking the beach and peered down at the rocks as waves washed over them. Wedged in between two large rocks was a white sign that appeared as if it were ripped from a large box, with a handwritten message in black Sharpie: "Pray, it helps." It served as my reminder that Allah (swt)—and communion with Him—was accessible to me from any city or town I might find myself in. And, perhaps, that I would need to be especially careful—and prayerful—here.

My first Saturday was more than welcoming. I found myself at a small, private studio, assisting Hollywood star Taraji P. Henson as she recorded the audiobook for her forthcoming memoir. For the next two years, I cruised through the city by scooter—from Orange Theory and yoga classes to courses at the SAE Institute for audio engineering and professional training at the CRE8 Music Academy, where I was learning the art of producing Billboard hits from a Grammy-nominated engineer and producer. And though I spent most of my days chasing the shadow of my dreams—weekly oud, guitar, piano, and singing lessons, recording music again, acting in short films, and signing with a talent agency—I still had to make ends meet. So, after leaving my job at Live Nation, I consulted school districts and large nonprofits. The culmination of my dreams was near. Or so I thought.

When I began releasing music again after a six-year hiatus, the reception was polarizing. Some posted sing-along videos of my songs on social media. Others accused me of hypocrisy for using my platform to share music alongside daily Quran videos. Now thirty, I had developed a thick skin that was only thickened by the loss of my father—though my heart was only more softened by his absence. I couldn't avoid the questions that pricked my conscience: *Are you **sure** the critics are wrong? Do you **actually know** what's right? Or are you too afraid to do the research and potentially upend your life?* What I *did* know is that God neither requires nor forbids something unless it serves to help us, heal us, and bring us "home." So, the search began.

Weeks of *dua* and many hard looks in the mirror left me with a simple yet profound realization: if I wanted to reach my truest potential, I would need to surrender my dreams to God and keep asking *Him* to reveal my path, instead of deciding that for myself. The more I surrendered, the louder and clearer the voice grew through the silence in my soul: *Come home, and pack light.* I listed and sold my furniture on Facebook Marketplace and OfferUp and brought two duffle bags of clothes home to Dearborn after a fourteen-year hiatus. I bearhugged ATM at the airport and thanked him for being a great brother and roomie (and for keepin' the sink clean). It was the most difficult transition of my life—especially since I left my instruments, and twelve years of musical dreams behind, too. In retrospect, I realized that my affinity for L.A.—a city of wanderers in search of answers and significance—mirrored the reality of my journey. I had yet to return to my roots. I had no idea what awaited; but I sensed that a homecoming—in its truest form—was on the horizon.

Not long after I arrived home to Dearborn, I received a text message from a former classmate at Emory. She had organized a "letter to yourself" activity for the Class of '14 exactly five years prior, on that date. She collected each of our handwritten notes and promised to share them with us five years later. I did not calendar the forthcoming occasion and had forgotten about it and about the contents of the letter. Like everything else, it arrived in perfect timing:

"Dear Ali,

May you have grown five rich, enlightening years

deeper into Islam and more intimate with Allah (swt) upon reading this note. If you have lost a loved one, may their spirit be ever more alive within you. If you have failed and/or faltered, may you be ever more faithful and determined... May your patience have paid off... May you have increased your remembrance of the next world such not to become too consumed by this one."

I exploded into tears, shocked at how the words I had written about losing a loved one likely carried the spiritual knowledge of destiny, of Baba's passing, that Allah (swt) placed on my pen that day so that I might find comfort amidst the pain it would evoke five years later, and inspire me to carry forth Baba's spirit of advocacy, love, and piety.

Meanwhile, I was living at home with Mama and my sisters; and, now thirty-two, I was trying to determine where my path would lead me next. My sister Rima was enrolled in her MBA program and building her entrepreneurial ventures, including her Dearborn Girl platform alongside her friends Yasmeen and Malak, who visited our home often. For months, Malak and I exchanged pleasantries and the occasional conversation about Islam, hijab, Dearborn, or one another's creative interests. I had only recently become open to the thought of marrying a woman who wore hijab—an openness that quickly evolved into a wish as my commitment to Islam grew.

My reflections on hijab became the other Harvard education I never knew I needed, for its meaning, its mischaracterizations, and its controversy in society helped facilitate my growth and learning in our *deen*.[72] Malak's hijab—and the humble yet confident way she carried herself in it—inspired me to call upon the best version of myself. She showed me that modesty is freedom; and her hijab beckoned me home, deeper into Islam, where peace by way of submission, humility, and true love resided.

Dearborn High's 2019 homecoming football game was against Fordson. Malak, despite growing up on the east side, was a Dearborn High girl. And of course, I'm a Fordson boy and fan who tries to finesse my way onto the sidelines like I did that night. I knew Malak would be there photographing the game, and I found myself looking around for her, wondering where she was. That homecoming game was symbolic—it was the day I discovered the feelings I had for her. A sign of a new beginning.

My nerves erupted as I carried a box of dates to her doorstep to meet her parents for the first time. As I approached the door wearing Baba's black polo sweater, I found peace in the same words he shared from Imam Ali (as) before my Harvard interview:

> *"Mountains may move from their position, but you should not move from yours. Grit your teeth. Lend to*

---

72   Religion.

Allah your head. Plant your feet firmly on the ground as though nails have been driven into them. Enter with a firm determination that you have lent yourself to the cause of God. With all this, remember, success lies in the hands of God."

It wasn't my parents' home, but entering that door felt like the truest homecoming I had ever experienced—a return to self. I would cry many times that night—including in front of Malak's family—and for many days after, for I was overwhelmed with feelings of gratitude to Allah (swt), as well as for how happy my mother was and is, and how happy and proud I knew Baba would be. And for being home—and healed—at last.

Three Years Later (2023)

I'm rushing Malak to Beaumont Hospital-Taylor amidst a health scare, and we're making *dua* on the road, begging Allah (swt) for mercy and asking Him to let His will be easy on us—whatever it might be. We're expecting our first child and given the circumstances that sent us there, it's only reasonable to prepare ourselves for the news of miscarriage.

The doctor enters the waiting room to whisper to the woman sitting near us—who is coughing vigorously—that she tested positive for COVID-19. We distance ourselves discreetly, relocating to the corner, waiting. When we're called in, the medical assistant does her thing: checking blood pressure and asking questions.

The circumstances are less than ideal for our first ultrasound—or so it seemed. We see our baby: heart beating fast, healthy, active. *Alhamdulillah* .[73] Malak's smile is unlike any I've ever seen on her face. Glued to the black and white screen, her eyes emanate utter joy. It's the unmistakable smile of a mother.

As we're preparing to leave, the physician double-checks with us:

"You guys know your due date?"

"Uh, we have an idea, but not yet, our appointment is upcoming." I said.

"Okay. Would you like to know?"

"Yes, please." Malak replied.

"Of course…it looks like…*March fourth.*"

We both figured the due date was likely to be around Baba's birthday, but seeing it fall precisely on the fourth sent chills down my spine. As the doctor walks away, Malak and I smile, our eyes watering. Humbled. Grateful. God willing, it's a good omen, that our daughter will carry forth the legacy her *jido* left. That she will embody his faith. And that she will take heed to the bold message that has defined him since birth: *Be free, child. And march forth.*

---

73   Praise be to God; often used colloquially as "thank God."

EPILOGUE

PRAYING

"Beware of the prayers of the oppressed, for there are no barriers between them and Allah (swt)."

-Prophet Muhammad (s)

One June afternoon in 2016, six years after his retirement, Baba marched excitedly into our dining room where I was seated with my laptop open for our third consecutive summer of transcribing his memoir into Microsoft Word as he paced back and forth, narrating stories. Our journey of writing this book began four years prior in early 2013. But finally, on this day, Baba stopped and looked my way with his signature smile and said, "Jig, I got the title."

I looked up and locked eyes with him, half excitedly, half skeptically, recognizing that unless it was *perfect*, I would have to kindly let him know, "Eh Baba, I don't think that's the one."

But as soon as he uttered it… *"The Prison of Minds…"*

I felt a strange feeling of shock and stillness as the words reverberated throughout my body, pulling the hairs on my arms to stand up against the gravity of the title's grim reality.

The irony in it was this: that despite the utter injustice behind the title, it filled me with a feeling of great hope for Fordson boys and girls. It offered me a brief respite from the sadness I felt over their condition. For as I sat there tasting my father's words, repeating them aloud to see if all the ingredients of a great title were in their proper proportion… *The Prison of Minds… The Prison of Minds…* I swam through the tides of being a Fordson Tractor: the innocent years of happy highs and harrowing heartaches, into years of lingering trauma and pain, into the present moment of a profound promise, a promise that in and of itself captured my transformation from a Fordson boy, trapped in a prison—then a prison of my mind—into a Muslim man, back home and basking in the freedom of a liberated spirit.

A wave of gratitude struck me: appreciation for Baba's grace, thankfulness for his tender love, and reverence for his bravery—both in that moment and in the lifetime leading up to it. I began to smile too, nodding, repeating, "*The Prison of Minds. The Prison of Minds*... It's perfect, Baba. It's *perfect*," I repeated, struggling to find the words to articulate why.

Eventually, what emerged was this: that only by calling Fordson what it is, could I begin to see the light from the dark cages it raised us in. In that moment, Baba's vision became my own. Because Mr. Fadlallah, all those years later, despite holding fast to the hope of freedom-at-last, knew all too well that although his love paid Fordson High a handsome visit, hate was our history, hate is here now, and hate is on the horizon. And only love imbued with knowledge and courage could overcome its forces.

Then, on "3.13," 2017, days after his 57th birthday, Baba passed.

For a year or two, I struggled with the question, "How do I complete *The Prison of Minds?*" Ultimately, I realized I could either publish his unfinished story or merge my story as a Fordson boy with Baba's memoir as Fordson's principal. Today, *March Forth* is a testimony about what it means to be an inmate in the prison of minds, to endure its aftermath, to lead through adversity, and to be a beneficiary of Imad Fadlallah's leadership.

But above all, *March Forth* is a call to action. It calls those of us who have graduated from Fordson and DPS to reflect on the good, bad, and ugly our public education has left us with; to ensure our successors aren't shortchanged as we have been for generations; to heal and grow closer to God; and to march forth in His cause. It calls those of us who are in DPS—students, parents, and staff—to *be* this change by demanding a high-quality, college-ready, and career-focused education, with adequate support for *all* children.

The actions we take should be as clear and bold as those taken by Baba—whether it was in the battlefield of hallways and classrooms or the eloquence of his emails and speeches. Among my favorite of these actions involved an email exchange between him and Dr. Artis, who was forced to investigate an allegation made by staff members that a counselor at Fordson High was running unauthorized after-school programs. This, the allegers claimed, was yet another example of Principal Fadlallah's "unethical practices"—and this allegation came after a series of others that accused Baba of favoritism, nepotism, and racism. Baba wrote the following:

> Dear Dr. Artis,
>
> Before I respond to the e-mail addressed to the board members and to you, allow me to clarify a few issues leading to my "unethical practices." Upon my arrival at Fordson, I spent a few weeks observing

and reflecting on the present practices and policies. I listened to parents, students, and staff. The first major obstacle was dealing with the number of self-appointed principals. The building engineer refused my directive to silence the fire alarm; the athletic director wanted to evacuate a gym filled with spectators during a basketball game without acknowledging my presence at the game. Over 300 students had to line up in the hallway for hours to obtain an ID; special education and bilingual students take the same required class up to five times, earning a G every time. On the other hand, counselors do not write letters of recommendations for higher achievers planning to attend competitive colleges or universities, limiting the boundaries of Fordson students to Henry Ford Community College, and discouraging students from pursuing their dreams.

Administrators hand out 10-day suspensions without intervention. Classroom management by many teachers was non-existent. Every time I eliminate a non-sense policy, I am faced with the side effects of being accused of favoritism, nepotism, and racism. When a new policy is instituted to improve teaching, and therefore, learning, I hear the same accusations.

I do not deny any of the upper "isms." I am waging a war on a culture of no expectations, disengagement, complacency, and bigotry (both faces).[74]

As far as favoritism, yes, I do favor the student who fell through the cracks, the student who remained faceless and nameless for four years and at times, five. The student who was met with only once when the counselor discovered he/she will not graduate. Nepotism? Yes, I do believe that every Fordson student is related to me, including "the 300 who come from Detroit,"[75] and I will treat each one the way I want my own children to be treated. Therefore, if believing in the advancement of every child is nepotism, I am guilty. As far as racism, again, I do have a soft spot for the underachiever. I am extremely biased when I encounter a failing student who is [being] failed by the mediocre practices of the system.

With all due respect, I applied the book of standards before anyone else in this district. Ten years ago [at Stout], I had at least one computer with internet access in every classroom, long before the district implemented technology, to allow all teachers easy access to the Michigan Curriculum. Seven years ago, my staff submitted weekly objectives based on the state standards and benchmarks that were posted on the school's website. Common assessments and teacher

---

74   By "both faces," Baba was referring to the covert/discreet bigotry, which he called "soft bigotry," as well as the blatant bigotry—both of which were (and remain) rampant within DPS.

75   Reference to a racist remark made by a staff member.

collaboration became embedded in the building culture. Book clubs raised the level of conversation from chewing gum and being unprepared, to dissecting and implementing best practices. My test scores speak very loudly to such practices.

I am insulted every time I have to respond to an anonymous inquiry about my "unethical practices." I am tired of being placed under the microscope. On the other hand, none of the inquiries submitted so far address the real problems:

Why is Fordson a failing school? What steps have been taken to address this failure? What are the obstacles in the way? Is there a culture of no expectations? Are the administrators aware of best practices and are they implementing them? What can we do to restore this educational beacon?

Unless... it does not really matter at this time? There is no need to invest in Fordson since the demographics have changed and parents' accountability is almost non-existent?

With my utmost respect sir, I will continue giving this task my relentless effort, dedication, and will. This is no longer about Fordson; it is about the entire community that has been shortchanged for years. I am honored that both of my sons are Fordson graduates; my daughter is a ninth grader, along with the rest of my extended family who attend and attended Fordson. I will never hide my dissatisfaction toward mediocrity and bigotry in teaching practices. I will never forget that [Mrs. X], a former counselor at Fordson, told my sister Insaf: "Do not bother with college applications; you are not going to college." Insaf is now a very successful pharmacist. I will never forget that my current assistant, who was then a counselor, told my sister Rima the same. Rima is a resource teacher at Lowrey, and a very good one if I may say so.[76]

For any staff member attempting to shortchange any of my students unwillingly, I will gladly show him/her the right way. If they choose to do it willingly, I will not be distracted nor misguided by the smoke they emit along the way as they attempt to cover their crimes against the human mind.

Regardless of the cost I will endure on a personal level, I will continue with my "unethical practices" of working toward this noble goal of leaving no child behind. I will continue making people examine their inner-soul and face their shortcomings. I will continue to make sure every child counts.

Now, I will answer your e-mail question. Before I even look into the situation, I will say yes, it is true. Somewhere in the counseling department, there is a counselor who does not leave until 6:00 pm or 7:00 pm; yes, she keeps students after school to help them and guide them; yes, she may be guilty of promising

---

76   Rima, or Mrs. Younes, is now Principal of Lowrey; and a very good one, if I may say so.

students that if he/she completes certain tasks, she will speak to the administrator about credit for community service; yes, she may have realized that the system shortchanged the student in the past and she is making up for it. And yes, she is the first Arab counselor in the history of Fordson.[77] What caused this? I met with the counselors a month ago and I spelled out my expectations—my very clear expectations about how to make every student count.

If you are going to respond to this person who cares so much about Fordson, please let me know. This is only a drop in my bucket.

Since early 2020, I've been teaching a course called College Success at Henry Ford College twice per year in the fall and winter semesters. My sections are reserved for students at Fordson High who are dually enrolled, most of them gaining

---

77   Reference to Ms. Nuzmeya Elder. Her heart wrenching email response to these allegations detailed the nature of support she provided for struggling or ambitious students, and their parents, as well as the utter failure of Fordson's counseling department in sharing this load. Despite her valiant efforts, she was forced to defend herself with statements such as: "I do not have an after-school program, do not offer classes after school, and am not authorized to offer such a program. More importantly, I do not have the time. I have never left students unattended in my office and am not engaged in any unethical practices and will not."

their first experience in a real college course. I emphasize to my students that the core qualities of college success are no different than the qualities required for life success; that if we can begin the work today of building the self-awareness, faith, curiosity, knowledge, and character we need to succeed in life, then success in college—or in anything else—will follow.

Our semester is filled with dialogues that transcend an otherwise limited college-prep curriculum. We discuss, in essence, the contents of *March Forth*—the Arab/Muslim identity, the concept of internalized oppression, the incident involving Coach Oss and Ali Houssaiky, the Dearborn Public School system, and the state of Fordson High today.

My students and I—for the most part—agree that the Fordson we observe today is much different than the Fordson that many teachers, administrators, and board members describe; for many of these adults love to remind us that Fordson and Dearborn Public Schools have "changed for the better." I am happy to admit, they're right.

To belittle the progress made at Fordson High is to ignore the fact that Imad Fadlallah grabbed it by its ankles and held it upside down, shaking its foundation until change fell from its greedy pockets. He redistributed those resources to the educationally bankrupt boys and girls who were starving to be taught, seen, and loved. He changed the way Fordson kids see themselves. He changed the way many *teachers* see themselves—from flustered babysitters to empowered educators who set high expectations. He changed how these teachers see their students—as capable of meeting and exceeding these high standards. He instituted a culture that the Class of '05, and any who came before us, couldn't even dream of—a culture where attending top colleges felt possible, then probable. A culture that continues to produce elite students and student-athletes achieving at the highest collegiate levels.

But many take "change" a step further to insist, "Fordson is no longer close to what it was in your day, Ali. Things are *much* better!" They cite the graduation rate of 95%—which only belies the reality: Fordson High's current math proficiency is 33%, while its reading proficiency is 39%—compared to the district's 56%.[78] In other words, it's easy to pass and graduate kids; it's a lot harder to make sure they're ready for college and careers.

In fact, according to GreatSchools, less than one out of three Fordson graduates (29%) even *attend* a four-year college or university within six months of graduation.[79] Sure, this statistic is skewed by the fact that many of them attend two-year colleges like HFC (46% do that instead of attending a four-year college). But consider this: among all students who attend any college, including two-year colleges, less than three out of four of them (71%) return to college for their second year.[80] This is not a surprise, since our college readiness score, according to *U.S. News & World Report,* is 20.3/100. The district average

---

78 2023 statistics. "Fordson High School." *U.S. News and World Report.*

79 2022 statistics. "Fordson High School." *GreatSchools.*

80 2022 statistics. "Fordson High School." *GreatSchools.*

is even worse—12.4/100.[81] So, in summary, less than two out of five students from FHS are proficient in reading. One out of three are proficient in math. And one out of five is college-ready—all according to our most recent statistics. You tell me: what story do the numbers tell?

Still, some educators or community residents tell a different story. They tokenize our outliers as a way to minimize this crisis. They cite the high number of Arab teachers or leaders as if to suggest that these leaders are champions for our children, when in fact—with some exceptions—most of them are safeguarding the status quo. Most dangerously, they proclaim that all bigoted guards and wardens in the prison of minds are gone, when in fact, many of these teachers and leaders—from the smart board to the school board—remain standing strong, poisoning our children's futures.

The claim that Fordson is far ahead of its history is not only false—it is dangerous. It is a lie that many are filled with desire or political motive to believe. The truth is, Fordson remains on the cusp of a failing public high school, even with a 95% graduation rate that disguises the lack of math, literacy, and real-world skills our graduates have. Fordson—and Dearborn Public Schools at-large—remains desperate for a makeover. And there would be no greater insult to the children and families Imad Fadlallah fought for than to claim that Fordson isn't a familiar monster today: in few ways better, in

---

81   2023 statistics. "Fordson High School." *U.S. News and World Report.* These scores are up slightly from 2022, when Fordson's college readiness score was 19/100, and the district's score was a 10.6/100.

more ways the same, and in many ways worse.

In November 2021, before I had ever referred to Fordson High as a prison of minds, my then student Abrar summed it up in this manner: "This place is really like a prison. Adults are always yelling at you, taking their frustration out on kids, trying to control and police our bodies. It's a very tense and aggressive atmosphere. You can tell that administration cares foremost about pleasing staff and treats students as if they're stupid."

Mohammed chimed in: "If you think about it, it really doesn't make sense. They tell us we need to grow up and be adults; that when we're eighteen, that's it, we're on our own. And yet, here we are, many of us just one month shy of eighteen, and they treat us like our opinion and thoughts have no value. I don't get it; what's going to happen magically in one month that they're suddenly going to respect me like the adult who they say I am?"

Finally, I realize many feel that the children—or at least their parents—should be held accountable for problems related to behavior or academic achievement. While I acknowledge and respect the role of parenting and accountability, I'll lean on the wise words of Mark Moore, one of my Harvard professors, who once said to my classmates and me, "Never forget, folks, that any society, any system, including school systems, will produce the exact type of citizen—behavior, morals, achievement—it was designed to produce. There are outliers, of course; but children, for better or worse, are the result of a system design, and the system doing *exactly* as designed.

So, if you don't like what you're seeing…well, don't blame the byproduct, don't blame the kids…you better reexamine the production line—the system at-large."

I'll rest my argument on that note. But before I rest my pen, I want to turn it back to Baba with a foreword he had prepared for *The Prison of Minds* that I have repurposed as part of this epilogue. And finally, I will leave you with some gratitude.

Dear Reader,

I wrote this book to make good on my promise to tell the untold story of Fordson High, with hopes that you will comprehend the magnitude of the problem in our local community and in our present education system.

The internet is rich with propaganda that perpetuates one story without due process and fairness. Many of the cases referenced here, including the many lawsuits brought against me, are legally documented and publicly accessible. I encourage you to google them if it would help you appreciate how deeply-seated the bigotry in our community is.

Students: above all, I owe this to you, the student leaders who taught me that the highest goal for an administrator is to demolish boundaries placed—voluntarily or involuntarily—upon you. It was you who rebelled against the status quo and asked the critical questions, often obvious questions that forced me to reflect upon my beliefs and dig deep into the trenches of our institution to find answers.

Parents: *The Prison of Minds* demonstrates how critical your role is in shaping the lives and futures of our children, as well as shaping school policies that will impact our community's children for years to come. I honor you for the sacrifices you've made and encourage you to trust our system less and monitor it more.

Teachers: For two decades, those of you who were committed to serving our children and families allowed me to stand on your shoulders to place the needs of students above your needs or anybody else's. I hope *The Prison of Minds* exemplifies the way some of you broke the prison doors open. Because of you, minds leapt over fences—imaginary fences that became too real when students were told again and again (and eventually convinced) that the barriers to access and opportunity were too high. To you I owe this book—not to validate what you do, or even to thank you for the selfless work you've done, but above all to say, *I feel you.*

Administrators: To those of you who have devoted your lives to providing a quality and equitable education for all children—I honor you. I honor you who believe it is our sacred duty to figure out how to reach every child; you who believe that each and every child can and will learn. Although at times it seems like a thankless job—as lonely and dark as a prison cell—I hope *The Prison of Minds* assures you that in due time your light reaches many, and that the return on your investment pays dividends of the most rich and noble kind. I'll leave you with four simple yet powerful questions that Dr. Artis once shared with us at a general administrator's meeting, based on the research of Richard DuFour:

    1) *What exactly do we want kids to know?*

    2) *How do we know that they know?*

    3) *What will we do if they don't know?*

Dr. Artis wisely added a fourth:

    4) *What will we do if they already know?*

My Family: I honor the amazing role that my beloved wife, Sawsan, and my four children played in helping to empower me to fight on behalf of other families and children. Although I put you on hold for those six years at Fordson, I always knew in my heart that you were central to this noble goal, and you were the support system that kept me standing firm amidst the tornado of Dearborn Public Schools.

-Imad Fadlallah, Dearborn, MI

Gratitude

Thank you Allah (swt) for creating me, and for blessing me with loving parents with giving hearts, and for blessing me with the lineage of *Ahlul Bayt*[82] (as) through the line of Imam Hassan *Al-Mujtaba* (as), whose virtues and divine leadership transcend what is visible to humanity, and who served as the perfect predecessor for an imperfect man like my father, who willfully and patiently embraced the assignments you gave him, and who always preferred to work for your pleasure behind the scenes and in secret. Thank you, Allah (swt), for Your infinite love, grace, wisdom, mercy, and supply of all things good—including all the blessings You bestow upon my daughter, my wife, me, and our families, especially those blessings we take for granted, for as You say in *Surah An-Nahl* and *Surah Ibrahim*, we can never enumerate them. I beg for Your forgiveness for my shortcomings: past, present, and future, including in this book. I am forever humbled and grateful to be guided, and I pray You keep me in the company of those You reference in 6:125 of the Holy Quran: "Whomever Allah wills to guide, He opens their heart to Islam."

---

82 Literally: people of the house. Refers to Prophet Muhammad (s), his holy daughter Fatima Al-Zahraa (as), her husband Imam Ali (as) (the commander of the faithful), their holy sons Imam Hassan and Imam Husayn (as), and their holy descendants.

Thank you, Mama, for your love and resilience and for being my best example of how never to fall into the trap of "minor polytheism" that Rasul Allah (s) fears for us, the trap we often fall into unknowingly when we place the perception others have of us—and our desire to be validated by other human beings—above our desire to be validated only by Allah (swt), and therefore above what is true and good. Thank you for editing and re-editing my book, with care and enthusiasm. Thank you for modeling diligent study of Quran even when you have your doubts or questions, and for being a great mama, and for being you—the woman Baba loved so dearly. Finally, thank you for being the best version of yourself in the final days that Baba lived; to honor him, comfort him, dignify him, and support him as he made his transition.

Thank you, Malak, my angel, my beautiful wife, for your support with *March Forth*, for helping me choose the new title, for writing the back-cover blurb, for designing countless mock-ups of the cover, and for teaming with my mama to edit and proofread my work so diligently. You're the best editor I know. What you did for *March Forth* mirrors what you do for me—you helped it reach its truest potential. Most importantly, thank you for your commitment to *Sirat Al-Mustaqeem*, including by fulfilling your end of a soulmate relationship with all your beautiful soul. Thank you for being a dedicated and loving wife and mother, and always desiring for yourself and us that we grow closer to Allah (swt).

Thank you to my siblings for your continued love despite my shortcomings. Mahmoud, thank you for sending me a life raft when I was drowning in Dearborn. Baba and Mama were great lifeguards, but I was swimming in a different pool when they were on duty. And though you were in Minnesota and could've easily ignored it, you stepped in to perform the labor of love required to pull me out.

Meme, in Chapter 8 (*Stupid*), I say that many of the adults who fought for me had to do so by fighting me. I think that best describes our relationship, too, for many years. Thank you for fighting for me in the best way you knew how, and I'm sorry for the impact that my mental health struggles had on your mental health. May Allah (swt) strengthen you and Ahmed and your union, through Islam, where all good—in this world and the next—awaits.

Sese, at your core, you are a content soul. I remember, almost two decades ago, watching you get your hair braided on I-forget-which-Caribbean Island we were on, when me, you, and Meme went on that cruise together. Your back was to me, and I kept hearing you sniff, quietly. Eventually, I suspected you were crying. I peeked around so you couldn't see me and saw tears trickling down your cheeks to your chin. You cried the entire time, and my heart was bleeding. But I kept thinking, *even her cry is modest.* You were always a symbol of delicacy and the fact that sensitivity is strength. And that shyness and silence can be freeing. May Allah (swt) guide you and our family.

Thank you to my grandparents, *Sayyed*[83] Mahmoud and

---

83   A title assigned to direct descendants of the Prophet Muhammad (s) through his *Ahlul Bayt* (as)

Fatimah (Oum Imad), may Allah (swt) rest your souls and reward you tenfold for your sacrifices and good deeds. Thank you for the well of love that never dried even as I drank from it endlessly. Thank you to my grandparents Nabih and Lila. May Allah (swt) grant you continued health and many more years of opportunity to earn His grace, mercy, and blessings. To Teta Lila: thank you for being such a loving *teta*, and for being Baba's biggest fan, the same way he was yours. When I see you frown with sadness at the mention of his name, I feel him smiling at you, and I hear him calling to you, "Don't worry."

Thank you to my aunts and uncles, paternal and maternal, whom I love dearly, for your love and guidance since my youth, and to your spouses. Thank you all for your support and admiration of Baba, so that others were inspired like you to see him as a light of truth and an example of *eman*[84] that he was and is. A special thank you to Amto Rima whose feedback on *March Forth* played a major role during the home stretch. And to Rima's bestie, Fudwa, my honorary aunt. Aside from your great feedback, too, what I'm most thankful for is something I never told you, and will never forget: the way you worked 12+ hour shifts in silence at our home after Baba passed, as hundreds of people circulated in and out—washing dishes; mopping floors; serving coffee, tea, and dates; passing out napkins to mourners; ordering food; all while staying under the radar and protecting our privacy, like an ever-present but invisible angel.

Thank you to my cousins who each had a special rela-

---

84   Faith.

tionship with Baba—especially Ahmed whose tech-savviness resulted in the discovery and use of critical excerpts and articles utilized in *March Forth* that Baba had stored away on countless hard drives. I know Baba would laugh at the fitting and irreplaceable role you played in helping to bring this book to completion. And to my cousin Hussein F., thank you for being my light back to *Ahlul Bayt*.

Thank you, ya Ibrahim. I call Baba my best friend, but he would have called me his son. It is obvious to anyone who knew him that he would have reserved the title "best friend" for you. I never fully understood the *hadith* of Imam Ali (as) when he said, "A friend cannot be considered a friend until he is tested on three occasions: in time of need, behind your back, and after your death." Your actions taught me why all three of these stages were important. May Allah (swt) bless and protect you and your family and reward you for all that you've done and continue to do.

Thank you to my parents and sisters by marriage, Hajj Wesam, Hajji Maram, Riyanne and Shereen, my newest and closest friends, for your warm embrace of me as a new son and brother, and for being a source of constant love and support, and for beautiful, shared memories that *inshaAllah*[85] will continue to grow. To Roro and Shesho, thank you for helping us brainstorm book-cover ideas, for being early readers, for providing critical feedback (like insisting on a hardcover version!), and for being so encouraging and excited throughout this process.

---

85   God willing.

Thank you to my daughter, Bayan. I can't believe how much I love you before meeting you. And how much you're already humbling me from the womb. If your kicks melt my heart, what will your cries, smiles, and words do? May Allah (swt) let us live to see.

Thank you, Baba, ya Imad. You inherited the name Sayyed by Allah (swt)'s blessing of lineage, and you proved yourself worthy of its title through your selfless sacrifice that so many—myself among them—are indebted to. Thank you for being my loving yet strict principal, twice. Thank you for being my generous father and my best friend. Thank you for embodying the words of Prophet Muhammad (s) when he says, "A father gives his son nothing better than a good education"—for you guided me back to Allah (swt) by way of Rasul Allah (s) and his Holy Progeny (as), the true sources of knowledge and education.

Thank you for teaching me to pray and teaching me *Surah Al-Fatiha*, and *Surah Al-Ikhlas*, which I recited aloud on repeat as I stood over you on that hospital bed, watching you endure the torment of recovery as you tried to rip yourself free from the machines and straps, overwhelmed by pain, while I was overcome with both my utter fear and complete faith in Allah (swt). Those two *surahs*[86] were all I knew then and all I could offer you—but I know this offering was mighty in the eyes of Allah (swt).

Thank you, Baba, for some of the last words I recall from you, after you were home recovering, when I informed you that I was competing to be the commencement speaker at

---

86 Chapters (Quranic).

Harvard. I told you, "I really think I'm going to win this one, Baba." And you replied in the most loving, convicted tone I ever heard you speak with: "You've already won, habibi. You've already won. Do you understand? Regardless of the outcome, it doesn't matter. You've already won."

I knew you were telling me that what I chose and was chosen for—Islam—would bless me far beyond any stage could ever begin to bless me with. And later, when I wasn't chosen for the speech, I realized that I wrote it only so that I could gain the victory of you speaking those parting words into my life, as if pointing me to the victory in *Surah An-Nasr* from the Holy Quran:

> "When the ultimate help of Allah comes, and victory is achieved,
> and you see people embrace Islam in crowds/droves,
> then glorify the praises of your Lord and seek His for-giveness, for surely, He is ever accepting of repentance."

May Allah forgive us both, and may we meet again, joyously, *ya Rab*.

Finally, thank *you*, my dear reader. Allah (swt) knows I struggled tremendously with this project over the last decade. If not for you, I would have lost the sense of purpose and drive I needed to finish this book. Please, if you are able and willing, pause to recite *Surah Al-Fatiha* (or your own prayer) for the souls of all the deceased mentioned in this book, beginning with *salawaat ala Muhammad wa ale Muhammad*.

BABA'S SPEECH

A speech I found in the inset pocket of Baba's
suit jacket, days after he passed away.

Trustees of the Board

Colleagues

Brothers and Sisters

Assalamu Alaikum. May peace be upon you all.

My son just completed the second year of his doctoral program in educational leadership at Harvard. Entering Harvard is a competitive dream to graduates from this community. Among over 800 applicants, Harvard selects 25 students for this program—all on scholarship, I should add. Last year, my son invited me and his mom to attend the "Change the World" seminar at Harvard, and I had the opportunity to actually chat and see the faces of people whose books I've read and never knew what they look like—think-tanks like Elmore, Gardner, and City.

Ali introduced me to several of the professors, and I attended a few of his classes. Dr. Jewell-Sherman, one of the professors, who was [also] on the interviewing committee, bragged about what an impressive young man Ali is [and] shared with me what tipped the scale and admitted Ali into Harvard.

It wasn't only his BA degree with honors from the University of Minnesota. It wasn't his graduation speech. It wasn't that he served in the most underserved town in America—Clarksdale, Mississippi—teaching high school English in the

Teach for America Program. It wasn't that he completed his master's degree in education while teaching. It wasn't that he had just finished his MBA from Emory University in Atlanta...

Ladies and Gentlemen: it was a letter his high school English teacher wrote about Ali's character. A letter from his English teacher that tipped that scale. Don't ever underestimate your power and your impact on children, on their lives, on their future.

Ali decided to host a trip to Lebanon for the Harvard cohort. I was volunteered to arrange the logistics: visiting the Minister of Education; the Lebanese University; and several schools, public and private. One of the schools we visited this past January was Al-Kawthar High School, one of the largest Islamic schools in Beirut. Walking down the halls, [Ali's classmate] Kim stopped me to ask me about a picture on the wall of a lady in a veil carrying her son and sitting under a palm tree. She asked, "Imad, what is this, and what does it say?"

I said, "It is a drawing by a student celebrating the birth of baby Jesus. It says the following:

Place of birth: Beit Lahm

Date of birth: 25th, Dhu Al-Qadah

His mother: Virgin Mary

The tree he was born under: Palm Tree

Extraordinary accomplishments: spoke at birth, raised the dead, and healed the sick."

Kim had tears in her eyes. She said, "I never knew that Muslims believed this about Jesus." I said, "Jesus is mentioned by name 25 times in the Quran and Mary 34 times. Prophet

Muhammad is mentioned 4 times by name."

So, if I did not grab onto this teaching opportunity, the drawing on the wall would have remained just a mother and a child under the palm tree. How many opportunities do you encounter on a daily basis to bridge the gap and strengthen understanding?

With this, ladies and gentlemen, I would like to take our conversation to the next level.

Teachers in our community—and I don't mean Arab and Muslim teachers—but *all* teachers in this community bear a huge responsibility. We live in an era of racial and cultural unrest fueled by ignorance and political ambitions.

While we face an educational achievement gap in public education, the racial and cultural gap is widening in America. I'll never forget the one time I walked into the office of Fordson High School in the eighties as a teacher, and I witnessed the Assistant Principal Mr. [Cali] yelling at a kid: "Look at me when I talk to you!" And the kid looks down at the floor. I waited until it was over, and I approached Mr. [Cali] and told him, "Looking down is the utmost form of respect. When a parent or a person of authority speaks to us and we look them in the eye, it is, in our culture, a form of disrespect."

Teachers in this community have learned many similar lessons about how and why we do what we do. Teachers in this community are the ambassadors of bridging the cultural gap. Teachers in this community are the guardian angels of the system and the safety buffer that prevents racism and ignorance from infiltrating our community.

Ladies and Gentlemen:

Teaching institutions are facing the largest decline in enrollment in decades.

The teaching profession is facing pay cuts after pay cuts.

School districts are struggling to stay afloat.

Teacher accountability for student achievement is increasing every year.

And amid all this and more, you are expected to teach. And today I am going to ask you to add to your plate…

I remember when I was the new vice principal at Stout Middle School. A student wanted lunch despite not having their lunch card and students being reminded repeatedly to have it on-hand. I told him he would need to remember to bring it next time. Lydia Lerini, who ran the kitchen, walked out to the cafeteria area, grabbed me by the shirt, and said, "Come here, young man, you follow me." Shocked, I followed her into the kitchen, where she showed me where the food is made and pointed to the large circular garbage cans. "Do you have *any* idea how much food we throw away each afternoon? For some of these kids, this is the only good meal they will have all day. Don't you *ever* turn a kid away from that."

"Yes, ma'am," I replied.

I learned from Lydia that essential human needs are far more important than a man-made rule.

I recall during my time as principal of Fordson High when I was preparing to suspend a student, Richard, for possessing and selling marijuana on school grounds. I told Richard he would be suspended for 10 days and that I would have to make a police report. He told me, "Go ahead, suspend me, she comes home drunk at 4:00 a.m. My twenty-four-year-old brother is going to beat the hell out of me, and the refrigerator is empty. Go ahead, suspend me."

I learned from Richard that I need to know and look at the whole child rather than simply following a code of conduct.

As a teacher, you have to be a good learner; you must learn from your students, from your colleagues, from your children, from your boss, from a book. Teaching is an ongoing learning process.

So, in many cultures, the word teacher is Al Murabi: s/he who cultures, raises, shapes, disciplines, educates.

Let us end with a challenge on facing the challenges we face: confronting racism, bigotry, drugs, alcohol, or inequity.

You are, in many cases, by far, the most stable environment a child has.

You are the gate to a bright future or a dark jail cell.

Let us do and not blame.

Let us accept the responsibility and not shift it.

Pause and learn; stop, and ask for directions—even the navigation is wrong at times.

I will leave you with a saying from Imam Ali (as):

"The humblest knowledge is what is expressed by the tongue, and the highest form of knowledge is what will appear on your extremities and facial expressions."

It is when you smile at a child.

It is when you listen with your whole body and not simply hear.

It is when you advocate. It is when you raise expectations.

It is when you guide and search for new ways to teach and reach.

You are the road map to the future. You are the light in a dark tunnel.

You are the hope for a hopeless child.

God bless you.

And thank you.

ABOUT THE AUTHORS

Prophet Jesus (as) said, "This world is nothing but a bridge into the afterlife."

Imad Fadlallah was an immigrant to Dearborn, MI who helped thousands of boys, girls, and families find firm footing on this bridge and *march forth.*

He was born on *March fourth,* 1960. *His birth* was a message.

He died suddenly on "3.13"—the area code of the community he marched for. *His death* was a message.

His name, *Imad Fadl-Allah,* means "*A firm pillar,* by the grace of God." *His life* was a message.

March Forth is his final message.

Ali Imad Fadlallah is a father, husband, writer, and college instructor. He is also the founder of Medina Media, an admissions company that supports applicants to college and graduate programs.

He earned an Education Leadership Doctorate (Ed.L.D.) from Harvard University, an MBA from Emory University, an M.Ed. from the University of Mississippi, and a BA in English Literature from the University of Minnesota.

He teaches at Henry Ford College, has previously taught at the High-Tech High Graduate School of Education, and has coached dozens of superintendents and education leaders nationwide.

He is also the voice of @14Pillars Podcast, where he aims to help us strengthen our relationship with the 14 Infallibles of Islam, one *hadith* (saying) at a time.

Printed in the USA
CPSIA information can be obtained
at www.ICGtesting.com
LVHW090120050324
773512LV00002B/153